The Aspiring Chef Learns to Cook

Written by: Anne Atkinson

Illustrated By: Pablo Quiroz

First class Press
1103 Middlecreek
Friendswood, Texas 77546
281-992-3131 TEL
www.mousegate.com
www.facebook.com/FirstClassPress
613-727-4723 ext. 5044

All rights reserved. Except as permitted under the United States Copyright Act of 1976, No part of this publication may be reproduced, stored in a retrieval system, or transmitted in any form or by any means electronic or mechanical or by photocopying, recording, or otherwise without prior permission of the publisher. Exclusive worldwide content publication / distribution by First Class Press and TotalRecall Publications, Inc.

Copyright © 2018 By: Anne Atkinson
Cover art and Illustrations: Pablo Quiroz
Copy editing and layout: Larry Cavanagh
All rights reserved

ISBN: 978-1-55323-603-0
UPC: 6-43977-45965-7
Library of Congress Control Number: 2018948954

Published in Canada by First Class Press
Printed in the United States of America with simultaneous printing in Australia, Canada, and United Kingdom.

FIRST EDITION
1 2 3 4 5 6 7 8 9 10

The scanning, uploading and distribution of this book via the Internet or via any other means without the permission of the publisher is illegal and punishable by law. Please purchase only authorized electronic editions, and do not participate in or encourage electronic piracy of copyrighted materials. Your support of the author's rights is appreciated.

Contents

Inspiration	iv-v
Basic Equipment for a Real Kitchen	vi-viii
No Stove Bare Bones Equipment	viii
Kitchen Tips for the Beginner	ix-x
Oven Temperatures	xi-xii
Electric Woks and Frypans	xii
Useful/and not Grocery Items	xiii-xiv
Basic Supplies	xv
List of Terms/Abbreviations	xvi-xvii
Imperial to Metric Equivalents	xviii
Breakfast	1
Veggies and Fruit	17
Salads, Sauces and Soups	43
Entrées	63
Sandwiches and Snacks	105
Sweet Things	121
Index	138

EATING IN: The Aspiring Chef Learns to Cook

You have a place to cook, a real kitchen or a spot in the dorm, some utensils and the motivation to eat in instead of out. Not only will you save tons of money, you'll also have fun developing cooking skills. Being in charge of your own food preparation is a challenging experience but completely worthwhile.

In this little book you'll find descriptions of methods and straightforward recipes for breakfasts, veggies and fruit, salads, sauces and soups, entrées, sandwiches and snacks, and sweet things. Some recipes come with tips to make shopping, storing and prepping easier. Some have instructions on how to achieve a complete meal. A few recipes are built upon prepared foods easily found in food markets. But do read their labels to check out fats and sodium levels! All recipes carry both imperial and metric measurements. Please read the page on imperial to metric equivalents and conversions.

Some recipes are suitable for bare-bones cooking facilities. They are labeled as SKILLET/El.WOK/FRYPAN, meaning that the dish can be prepared using either a stove or an electric wok or frypan. Other pages list essential tools for both bare bones and real kitchens.

The main advice this book offers the beginning cook is to be not afraid. Accidents happen. Toast burns, meat dries out, potato water overflows and so on. But when you are learning to feed yourself, what's the panic? Just remember to keep milk, ice cream, fruit and cereal boxes on hand. Together they make a meal and you won't starve.

Many people and written resources helped me along the way to this book. Chief among them was Jane Fulton, PhD, a nutritionist and a long time friend and colleague. I have tried to list below the names of all the others who tested recipes or offered advice. Included in the latter group are cooking experts from newspapers and TV, documented over the years on my scraps of yellowed paper and scribbled notes. I thank them all most sincerely.

Inspiration
Charlotte Brock
Margo McKimm
Food TV
Marjorie Horton
Mary Moore
Global economy after 2007

Testers and helpers
Aileen Moore
Allison White
Ann Gillies
Beth Atkinson
Carole Petrin
Ellen Lochead
Isabel Baker
Jackie Hill
Jean Wellington
Joan Flynn
Joan Newcombe
Jim Morwick
John Atkinson
Laurie Liberty
Lila Fraser
Lorene Morwick
Lynde Ewert
Margot Pallett
Marilyn Braden
Mary Duncan
Mary Margaret Lacompte
Murielle Cregan
Nancy Fowski
Peggy Flynn
Rachel Pink
Sandy Morrow
Sheila McKimm
Suzanne Roux
Terry Atkinson
Walter Fowski

Anne Atkinson, Manotick, Ontario, 2011

Basic Equipment for a Real Kitchen

Pots and Pans	small, medium and large saucepans
	non-stick skillets, 6"/15cm, 10"/25cm
	oven-safe 12"/30cm skillet
	non-stick stove top grill pan
	roasting pan with lid
	pasta pot/stock pot
	sturdy aluminum sheet pan with rims
	heavy roasting pan with rack
	9x13"/23x33cm oven pan &
	8x8"/20x20cm baking pan
	2 round 8" or 9"/20 or 23cm cake pans
	muffin tins
	glass pie plate
	loaf pan
	2 cookie (half sheet) sheets
	wok
Small Appliances	kettle
	slow cooker/crock pot
	food processor and or blender
	electric mixer
	microwave oven
	toaster or small counter toaster oven
	electric wok/electric frypan
Bowls	mixing bowls, various sizes
	refrigerator bowls with lids
	microwaveable bowls
	1 C/240ml & 4 C/1 L see-through measuring cups
	large colander/strainer

Small Tools	balloon whips/whisks, large and small spatulas, a variety of sizes and shapes wooden & silicone long-handled spoons soup ladle kitchen scissors 12"/30cm locking tongs for lifting can opener peeler (with thick handle) masher, preferably metal large and small sieves measuring spoons, 1/8 t-1T/0.65-15 ml small strainers/sieves silicone kitchen brush 3 sided grater steamer basket salad spinner cutlery for 8 serving spoons
Knives	paring – one serrated, one not chopping ('chef's' knife) carving (thin, long, sharp blade) curved and serrated for fruit
Boards and Mats	silicone/glass mats for chopping* wooden board with juice troughs** silicone mat for baking
Other Stuff	aluminum foil, parchment paper plastic wrap and food bags oven mitts and pot holders kitchen towels and dish cloths

*preferably different colours for different foods – for safety against bacterial cross-contamination
**for cutting breads and carving cooked meats

No Stove Bare Bones Kitchen Equipment

Small appliances
slow cooker/crock pot*
wide mouth electric kettle**
electric wok/frypan for use as a skillet
toaster/toaster oven
small microwave oven

Small ware
serrated paring knife
'chef's' knife
ladle
can opener
balloon whip
spatula
strainer
measuring cup & measuring spoons
cutlery for 2-4
serving spoon

Other stuff
heavy aluminum foil for use as a prep tray, lid, wrapper)
2 cutting boards***
baggies for food storage
plastic wrap for food storage

Crockery
small platter for prep and serving
2 bowls for prep and serving
place settings for 2-4

*to cook and/or heat up practically anything
**for beverages and soups
***one for uncooked meats, one for all other foods

Kitchen Tips for the Beginner

Boiling Water (!) is a must to soften fruit skins, to blanch veggies, to soften rice noodles and to make a proper cup of tea. A stove-top kettle or an electric kettle will boil water faster than a microwave.

Ice Cold Water is a must when making pastry and is just the thing to quick-cool veggies so that they do not continue to cook.

Cutting Boards are essential tools but they are also dangerous to your health. Almost any board, regardless of its material, tends to harbour bacteria that can harm you. An easy way to avoid problems is to use different boards for different foods. For example, use a red board to cut up chicken and turkey that are often sources of salmonella. Use a brown board for meats, a yellow board for veggies and fruit and a white board for bread. And always wash a board well after use.

Baking Soda is a kitchen staple because it has many uses. First, an open box of baking soda should be kept in your fridge to absorb odours that affect other food, e.g., blue cheese. Second, baking soda releases burnt bits from the bottom of a pot. Add 1/2 C soda to enough water to fill the burnt pot halfway and boil until the burnt bits float to the top. Then wash the pot normally. Third, baking soda can be useful in refreshing oft-used coffee makers and tea pots. There are a host of other uses for baking soda that you will discover over time, especially its use in baking as a leavening agent.

Vinegar is a must in any kitchen. It's an all-purpose cleaner that cuts grease, deodorizes and disinfects and it also provides the acid in many recipes such as salad dressings.

Measuring spoons now sold in Canada are usually calibrated for use in both the U.S. with its imperial system and in Canada with its metric measures. Small spoons may show slightly different amounts than in your recipe. For baking, since exact measures are important, it is best to use the imperial units of teaspoons, tablespoons and cups.

The diagram below shows the usual spoons ranging from the large 1 T/15ml to 1 t/5ml, to 1/2 t/2.5 ml to 1/4 t/1.25ml in the top row and the unusual added spoons ranging from the 'large' 1/8 t/0.65ml, to the small 'dash' and the smaller 'pinch' to the smallest 'smidgen'.

Measuring Cups suffer from the same deviations. In common use is a one cup measure that usually translates to 250ml. Yet the cup set sold in most Canadian hardware stores indicates an amount of 240ml for one cup. See page xviii on imperial to metric conversions.

Oven Temperatures

Full Ovens – in a range, built into a wall or free standing – are the norm in most kitchens. The natural temps of ovens vary depending on size, age, engineering and quality. Hence a small toaster oven delivers heat quicker and more directly to its food while a large wall oven's heating temp may be slow but can be augmented by using the convection setting so that heat is continually swirling around the food.

Generally, 350F/180C degrees in a large oven is the normal setting for roasting and baking (with the exception of the first 15 min bake for roasts and pastry at 410-425F/205-230C degrees). At 350F/180C, liquid inside the cells of the food heats and expands so cell break-down occurs. Each oven needs experimentation to get the temp setting just right. As you cook, you will know.

Microwave Ovens are everywhere. But they all behave differently. The heating capacity of microwaves depends on the oven's wattage. The higher the wattage the faster the oven cooks. You will need to adjust cooking times according to the oven you are using.

Toaster Ovens are great little appliances for making toast, baking foods such as potatoes, roasting small amounts of meats, reheating stews and finishing casserole dishes with crunchy tops. They do make for problems, though. Depending on a toaster oven's features, the toast setting may take forever. Yet the baking and broiling settings do a bang-up job. Do use them though because a toaster oven consumes less electricity than a full size oven.

Temperature Conversion Chart - Below is an approximate conversion chart between gas mark and electric ovens. It was copied from *the rec.food.cooking* FAQ.

Gas Mark	Fahrenheit	Celsius	Description
1/4	225	110	Very cool/very slow
1/2	250	130	---
1	275	140	cool
2	300	150	---
3	325	170	very moderate
4	350	180	moderate
5	375	190	---
6	400	200	moderately hot
7	425	220	hot
8	450	230	---
9	475	240	very hot

Electric Woks are featured in several recipes in this book. They make great cooking appliances for bare bones kitchens because they deliver heat ultra-fast to the centre of their curved bottom. And, food that is already cooked in the wok can be pushed up the curved sides to stay warm. However, the cook must experiment with the appliance to become familiar with the intensity of its heat at each temperature setting. You need to know where 'low', 'medium' and 'high' heats actually are on the dial of your electric wok.

Electric Fry pans are relatively old fashioned but still popular for many reasons. They heat quickly, use less electricity than a stove and do a decent job frying and a good job simmering. For "el.wok" recipes in this book you may use an electric frypan.

Useful/and not Prepared Grocery Items

Prepared Sauces with catchy names indicating a connection to the cuisines of Asia, India and other seemingly exotic parts of the world are now widely available. They are convenient but costly. They also have taste problems – most are too sweet or too salty or have a bitter/chemical after-taste. Better to make a simple sauce yourself if you have the time.

Canned Soups may also a problem. Although convenient, not overly costly and quite tasty, they are usually loaded with sodium (salt). But dried soups with low sodium labels are a decent product. Simply use a broth packet as your soup base and add real veggies and proteins from your fridge.

Tofu is now so common in Western diets that consumers may not even recognize this prepared soy product as part of a favorite dish. Think Pad Thai or Vegetarian Lasagna. Tofu has many virtues. Chief among them is its acceptance of the flavours of aromatics such as garlic and the sweet or sour or hot or salty sensations of onion, vinegar, chilis, and soy sauce. Tofu is sold in most grocery stores packaged as soft, medium and firm. In stir fries, medium tofu cubes can stand in for protein, creating a delicious vegetarian concoction.

Chopped Garlic in a bottle is a welcome staple for today's cook. Many of the savoury recipes in this book call for sliced or minced garlic. So having the peeling and chopping already done is a time saver – and your hands won't reek of garlic oil.

Peanut Butter has become almost a bad word because so many children (and adults) have peanut allergies. But for the cook who likes nuts, peanut butter should be thought of as a kitchen staple. It makes the tastiest quick sandwich, it melts down to form the base for sauces and dips, it is a common ingredient in squares, cakes and ice cream toppers and it is good for you! Two tablespoons of PB delivers 17% of our Vitamin E daily requirement, a powerful antioxidant that helps protect our bodies against chronic diseases.

Canned Beans come in many varieties these days. All are useful in soups, salads, stews, and pasta preparations. In this book recipes containing canned beans ask the cook to drain the brine from the beans before using in order to reduce the beans' salt content, which is usually high. However, you may want to rinse part and leave the brine on part of the total quantity of beans in order to retain the soluble fibre, minerals and thiamin in the can's liquid.

Prepared Salads! Are they an extravagance or not? If you are lazy about washing, storing, preparing and actually eating lettuces and other greens, then prepared salads are a good idea. They don't last long but they are ready for your meal. The packet of dressing can be used or saved for another purpose. And do not ignore the staple veggies in your crisper...add sliced carrots, cukes, celery, peppers, onions, cabbage and herbs to the prepared salad and you have an entirely different dish with more nutrients and flavour. Of course tomatoes are a great addition but they should NOT be stored in your fridge.

Ice Cream is found in most freezers. Did you know that ice cream <u>made with real cream</u> has uses beyond its frozen form? It can stand in for whipping cream by beating it, slightly thawed, in an electric mixer. Or, put the ice cream in a cold glass jar with a tight-fitting lid and shake it up for about 5 minutes. Good exercise! In its thawed form, vanilla ice cream can be used as Crème Anglais, a lovely sauce for puddings.

Basic Supplies – add to them as you cook!

<u>In your Pantry</u>
salt, pepper
white sugar, brown sugar
all-purpose flour
tea and coffee
rice, tortilla chips
potatoes, tomatoes
extra-virgin olive oil
pasta
quick cooking oatmeal
tins of tomatoes
tins of tuna, salmon
soy sauce
mustard
cinnamon
dried thyme leaves
dried basil

baking powder
baking soda
bouillon cubes
peanut butter
jam, honey
globe onions, carrots
vegetable oil
crackers
corn meal
canned beans
baked beans
garlic cloves
pickles/relish
nutmeg
dried rosemary
dried parsley

<u>In your Fridge</u>
milk and cream
butter, mayo
cheeses
eggs
yogurt

bacon
lettuce/greens
green onions
ginger root
lemons, apples

<u>In your Freezer</u>
bread (it does not go bad)
ice cream
meats, fish, fowl

veggies
orange juice
wieners

pizza bases/prepared pizza   sausages
left overs (labeled)   cheeses

List of Terms/Abbreviations used in this book

al dente	cooked until tender/'toothsome'
baguette	long, skinny French bread
bain-marie	shallow dish of water surrounding another pan, often custard
balsamic (vinegar)	sweet-sour aged Italian vinegar
BP	baking powder
BS	baking soda
blanch	quick cooking to set enzymes
braising	roasting protein/veg with liquid
C	imperial measurement, 1 cup = 8 fl oz /240ml or 225g
caramelize	slowly fry/sauté until golden
carb	carbohydrate
cream (verb)	mash together very well
crepe	flat, thin pancake
crème fraiche	soured heavy cream
croutons	crunchy cubes of bread
dash/pinch	a measure of less than 1/8 t/0.65ml
dredge (verb)	coat with flour (usually meat)
deglaze	dissolve browned bits in liquid
deveined	gastro-intestinal vein removed
Dijon	a French mustard
drippings	luscious liquid from cooked meats
el.wok	electric wok
EVOO	extra-virgin olive oil
fold (verb)	using a broad utensil, move an ingredient from the top to the bottom of a bowl and through

	another ingredient, thus incorporating the two
frites	another word for French fries
frittata	Italian style omelet with veggies
g	metric measurement of a gram
L or l	metric measurement of a litre
lemon grass	savoury grass used in Asian dishes
macerate	to soften by soaking in liquid
Make-a-Meal	suggestions for additional foods that will complement the recipe
marinara	pasta sauce of tomatoes + garlic
micro	microwave oven
min	minute
mL or ml	measurement of a millilitre
P	pepper
paint (verb)	using a kitchen brush, cover as if painting, eg., glaze a spare rib
pkg	package
polenta	fine yellow cornmeal/cooked mush
rasp	tool used to grate finely
S	salt
sec	second
SKILLET/El.Wok	use either skillet or electric wok
shock (verb)	quickly cool down using ice water
spatula	long handled flexible paddle
spider	long handled wire scoop
stock	a meat, fish or veggie broth
sweat (verb)	to soften (veg) using low heat
t	a teaspoon
T	a tablespoon
temp	temperature
TIP!	how ingredients/methods work
umami	the fifth category of flavor

vinaigrette	salad dressing of oil & vinegar
whip (verb & noun)	beat quickly with a fork/a whip tool
zest	the coloured portion of fruit rind

Imperial to Metric Equivalents/Conversions

A few words of explanation are needed on the subject of metric equivalents and conversions. In North America, the imperial measures that Grand Ma grew up with are still used in the U.S. Thus, for many printed recipes, they are still the only or the premier measure you will find. Canadians use both systems with varying degrees of fluency depending on their age. The young people who use this book will tend to think metric, while an older cook may depend on imperial measures.

Unfortunately, equivalents are something of a mystery. When different parts of the world converted from imperial to metric measurements, varying values were assigned to some metric measures. For example, the imperial measure of 1/2 teaspoon was converted in Canada to 2.5 millilitres, while in Australia, the conversion is 2 millilitres. Similar differences show up in weights. In Canada 2 ounces usually became 55 grams but 60 grams in Australia. Furthermore, conversion tables are inconsistent, tending to use either or both a 'soft' and 'hard' approach to metric measures, thus further confusing the equivalents.

<u>The cook usually can ignore minor variations in measures, except in baking recipes.</u> Try to use imperial measure recipes when ingredients are needed to create chemical reactions as in baking. The amounts of baking powder and baking soda needed to enable a buttermilk waffle to rise must be consistent to be correct. If not, failure to rise and an unhappy cook are

certain results. By the way, baking powder is nothing more than baking soda plus cornstarch. Still, a cook should always have on hand a <u>fresh</u> tin of baking powder.

El.Wok Recipes:	
Perfect Hard Boiled Eggs	4
Perfect Scrambled Eggs	6
French Toast	9
Your Own Oatmeal Porridge	13

Breakfast

Breakfast BLT	2
Baked Egg Plus on Toast	3
Perfect Hard Boiled Eggs	4
Perfect Poached Egg	5
Perfect Scrambled Eggs	6
Perfect Soft Boiled Egg	7
Eggs with Hash	8
French Toast	9
Easy Omelet	10
Anne's Blueberry Pancakes for 4	12
Your Own Oatmeal Porridge	13
Basil's Best Buttermilk Waffles	14
2 Eggy Sandwiches	16

Breakfast BLT

Here is a nutritious and delicious breakfast idea: a BLT open-faced sandwich with an egg on top (or a two-bread BLT with the egg inside).

Gather together:
1 English Muffin/hearty Bread/whole wheat Bagel
1 T/**15ml** Butter for buttering and frying
1-2 thin slices Cheese, preferably not processed
1 Egg
2 leaves sturdy Lettuce/Kale/Spinach
2 slices Bacon, cooked
1 small Tomato, sliced

Toast bread and fry egg:
Toast and, if desired, butter	your breads.
Top with	cheese slice.
In a skillet on med heat melt	butter
and when it sizzles, crack in your	egg.

Cover the egg with a pot lid and allow to cook until the yolk sets lightly, about 4 mins.

Construct your BLT:
Arrange on cheese toast	green leaves
	bacon
	tomato slices
	cooked egg.

Finish:
If using, gently press on top	the second toast

so that the egg yolk runs down into the sandwich.
Alternately, poke the yolk to allow it to run into the open-face BLT.

Baked Egg Plus on Toast

Here is a simple recipe for supper, lunch or brunch. The amounts below make an entrée for one. (For two or four servings just multiply the ingredients by 2 or 4.)

<u>Gather together:</u>
small ovenproof ramekin (an individual casserole dish)
1 T/**15ml** Butter, melted
1/3 C/**80ml** or so Prosciutto, Ham or cooked Sausage, chopped
1 T/**15ml** chopped Parsley
1 Egg
Salt & P
2 T/**30ml or more** grated Cheese
1 or 2 slices of Bread for toasting

<u>Turn oven or toaster oven to 350:</u>
Into the oven put a shallow pan half-filled with water (to make a "bain-marie").
<u>Fill up your ramekin:</u>
Butter your little dish and fill it with   butter, melted
                                                    chopped meat
                                                    chopped parsley.

Whisk together   egg
                                                    S & P

and pour into the ramekin over the meat.
Sprinkle the top with   grated cheese.
<u>Bake egg dish and toast bread:</u>
Carefully transfer the ramekin into the "bain-marie" that has enough hot water to go half-way up the sides of the dish. Bake about 20 minutes to cook egg. Toast one or two slices of bread, then slide the egg onto the buttered toast.

Perfect Hard Boiled Eggs STOVE/EL.WOK.FRYPAN

Eggs cooked by this method will be perfectly hard-boiled and will not have a grey ring around the yolk.

Gather together:
Eggs
Cold water
Saucepan
Bowl of ice-cold water

Carefully cook eggs:
In a saucepan/wok to fit the number you are cooking place eggs.
Cover eggs with cold water.
Bring water to a boil.
Place lid on saucepan/wok and remove pan from heat (turn off wok).
Let stand 10 minutes to finish cooking.
Drain eggs.

Crack, cool and peel:
Pick each egg out of the hot water with a wire spider or spatula with holes and crack the eggshell with the handle of a knife for easy peeling.
Place eggs in ice-cold water.
Peel shell away from the whites.

Cut or mash eggs:
Gently cut eggs into desired shapes (halves for devilled, thick slices or quarters as part of a salad plate).
Or make egg filling with mashed eggs, mayo, S & P, mustard, celery, onion.

Perfect Poached Egg

Some cooks have trouble poaching eggs. Here are a few secrets to success: Read on!

Gather together:
1-2 Egg(s)
1 small dessert Bowl
1 t/**5ml** mild Vinegar such as white or rice (unflavoured)
1 Shallow Pan with simmering Water
Large pierced Spoon or Spatula

Crack egg into bowl:
Using a knife, crack the eggshell and release egg into the dessert bowl.

Prepare the cooking water:
Put about 2 inches of water into a shallow pan.
Bring water to the boil then turn heat down to simmer.
Add to the simmering water vinegar.

Cook the egg(s):
Gently slide into the water egg(s)
Using spoon/spatula, continuously scoop water over top of the egg(s). Let cook about 4 mins until yolk is done to your liking. (You will have to experiment to achieve the correct time for you and your stove.)
Slide spoon/spatula under entire egg
and lift out of water, allowing water to drip away from egg.

Make-a-meal: Now it's up to you how your poached egg is eaten: On toasted bread, on corned beef hash or on its own.

Perfect Scrambled Eggs
STOVE/ EL.WOK.FRYPAN

Eggs scrambled by this method will be perfect – soft and creamy, melt-in-your-mouth!

Gather together:
Eggs, lightly whipped with a fork – **2** large eggs per person
Butter – 1 t/**5ml** per egg
Cream – 1 T/**15ml** per egg
S & P
the right size pot, e.g., small saucepan for 2 eggs and 10"/**25cm** skillet for 8 eggs OR use your el. wok

Heat the pan/el.wok, then the butter, then the eggs:
Heat the pan/el.wok on medium.
Add and allow to sizzle   butter.
Pour in all at once   eggs
and allow bottom of eggs to set.
Stir eggs lightly with a wooden spoon.
Stir in   cream.
Remove from heat as soon as eggs form lovely lumps but are still loose (eggs continue to cook off heat).
Sprinkle with   S & P.
Serve immediately.

Make-a-Meal: Scrambled eggs are usually eaten as part of a breakfast plate. But they can also be used as a sandwich filling or as a topping for a veggie concoction such as ratatouille.

TIP! Try adding savoury bits to your scrambled eggs. Chopped green onion, chopped peppers, sun-dried tomatoes, black beans, hard and soft cheeses, smoked salmon, sausage and ham are some suggestions.

Perfect Soft Boiled Egg

So easy to prepare and so good. If you have an old-fashioned 'egg cup' just slice off the egg's tip and dig in.

Gather together:
1 Egg
a Pot
cold water

How to boil water and cook an egg:
Fill a small pot half full of cold water.
Place in the pot the egg.
Heat the water until it boils
and keep it **gently** boiling for 4 minutes.

About Eggs: There are several kinds of eggs available to the consumer these days. Size: Common sizes are medium, large and extra-large. It's a good idea to usually buy size 'large', as they are standard in recipes. Colour: White is boring and brown is attractive and, therefore, more costly. There is no difference between them in nutritional terms. Nutrition: An egg's content depends of course on the food eaten by the hen. They can be fed to produce eggs containing Omega 3 oil, a super healthy nutrient. Free-range. Chickens allowed to run around the barnyard eating a variety of foods are labeled "free-range". Safety. If you are able to buy free-range eggs you will probably avoid the possibility of salmonella, a common problem with factory-raised chickens and eggs. Because of that, consumers are warned against eating raw eggs and urged to keep egg shells away from other foods.

Make-a-Meal: Egg on toast is a good meal at any time of the day and great with baked beans and sliced tomatoes.

Eggs with Hash
Here is an old-fashioned 'diner special' that makes a tasty and substantial supper.

Gather together:
1 T/**15ml** Oil **+** 1 T/**15ml** Butter
1 waxy (round or all-purpose) Potato, grated
1/2 Carrot, grated
1/4-1/3 C/**60-80 ml** Roasted or Corned Beef, shredded
S & P
1 Egg
dab of Butter
1 Green Onion, minced, for garnish

Fry away:
Heat a small skillet on med with   butter and oil.
When foam subsides, add   potato and carrots
pressing the veg lightly into a cake.
Sprinkle with   S & P.
Cover and cook for 5 mins.
Turn over with a wide spatula.
Sprinkle all over the cake   beef shreds.
Press down lightly so that the
meat is incorporated into the cake.
Cook, <u>uncovered</u>, another 5 mins.
Test for doneness by removing a
sliver from the centre of the cake –
if the potato shreds are tender,
the cake is ready for its egg. If not,
cook another 2-3 mins and test again.
Remove the cake to a warm plate.
Fry in the same pan with more butter   1 egg per person.
Arrange egg on cake & garnish with   green onion bits.

French Toast

SKILLET/ EL.WOK.FRYPAN

French toast is usually thought of as a breakfast dish. But it can also be a comforting lunch or the sweet finale to a dinner. This recipe is for 1 serving of two pieces of toast. Note that you will have egg custard left over. For 2 servings simply double the ingredients.

Gather together:
1 Egg
2 T/30ml Milk
1/2 t/2.5ml Vanilla
tiny pinch Salt
1 t/5ml Sugar
2 slices Bread, raisin, egg or home-style are best
1 T/15ml Butter
Maple Syrup
Optional: **1/2** Banana in large chunks + **1 t**/5ml Brown Sugar + **1 T**/15ml Butter

Prepare the custard:
In a shallow bowl beat together	egg, milk, vanilla, salt, sugar.
In the custard soak for at least 2 mins (turning slices over using a spatula).	bread slices

Fry the toast:
In a wide skillet/el.wok on medium melt	butter.
When foaming subsides, gently add	soaked bread.
Fry about 5 mins, until bottom is golden and then turn slices over and fry another 2 mins until bread is puffed and bottom has browned.	
Serve with warmed	maple syrup
or optional fried bananas with sugar.	

Easy Omelet

SKILLET/ EL.WOK.FRYPAN

Do not fall prey to the idea that omelets are tricky. They're not, when you follow the directions below. The diagrams should help you to turn out a lovely egg crepe with its filling firmly encased in a golden envelope.

Gather together:
2 Eggs
1 Green Onion, minced
1 T/**15ml** + 1 t/**5ml** Butter to finish the dish
1/4 C/**60ml** Shredded Cheese – cheddar, Monterey Jack
1/2C/**120ml** Tomato, seeded, diced (or your choice of veg)
S & P

Prepare the egg:
With a small whisk, beat lightly	eggs.
Stir in	green onion.

Cook the egg:
Heat a small skillet/el.wok on med-high.
Add and heat until bubbles subside	butter (1 T/**15ml**).
Pour in	egg mixture

and tilt the pan so the liquid egg runs underneath the solid egg.

Add the filling and fold the crepe into an omelet:
As soon as all liquid is gone, add in a line across centre of the crepe.	cheese & tomato

Immediately flip over 1/3 of omelet onto itself. (The filling will now be in the centre of the folded crepe.)
Now flip the other 1/3 crepe overtop.
Slide or flip the omelet onto a warm plate and spread it with	(1 t/**5ml**) butter.
Sprinkle with a bit of	S & P.

How to Fold an Omelet with Filling:

Anne's Blueberry Pancakes for 4

When blueberries are in season this recipe is a 'must make'. Alternatively, well drained frozen berries may be used all year.

Gather together:
Box of Buttermilk Pancake Mix
Buttermilk or Water, amount according to box instructions
+ Optional **1-2** Eggs, beaten
Melted butter, **2 T**/30ml at least
Soft Butter for frypan
1C/240ml Fresh Blueberries, washed & dried/frozen & drained

Prepare the pancake batter:
Follow the instructions on the box.
BUT, ensure that the mix contains egg
If not, add   1-2 beaten eggs.
Stir in   melted butter.
AND, preferably use for liquid   buttermilk, not water
to make the pancakes rich and fluffy.

Heat a large skillet & cook in three stages:
Use med or med-high heat, until a drop of water bounces right off the pan.
Add to the skillet and melt, swirling,   **1 T**/15mL butter.
Into the skillet place   **4** scoops of batter.
(Stage 1) Cook until bubbles begin to appear all over the tops.
(Stage 2) Sprinkle all over the tops   blueberries.
After 1-2 mins turn the pancakes – the bottoms should be golden brown.
(Stage 3) Reduce heat a bit and cook until blueberry syrup begins to ooze out from under the cakes.
Remove the cakes to a warm platter.

Your Own Oatmeal Porridge   SKILLET/ EL.WOK.FRYPAN

It's a snap to cook. And an easy dish to 'flavour up'. Use fruits, cinnamon or other homey spices, honey or brown sugar to sweeten, and you have your own morning special. Oatmeal has the added virtue of lowering LDH levels by upping your fibre intake. Also, it's filling and inexpensive.

Gather together:
1 C/240ml Water
2/3 C/160ml Rolled Oats (not instant!)
pinch Salt
optional: **1/2 t**/2.5ml Butter

Dump into the pot or el.wok, stir, boil, stir:
On the stove or in an el.wok put   water
                                          oats
                                          salt.
Stirring constantly, bring to a boil.
Lower heat and let oats thicken.
Stir in, if desired   butter.
Serve with milk or cream
and your own 'flavour up' additions.

TIP! The amounts of oats and water specified above are flexible. More water makes a soupy cereal, more oats a thicker porridge. Also, it isn't necessary to stick to rolled oats. Some grocers sell packets of mixed cereal grains for quick cooking. They are usually tasty and contain added nutrients.

TIP! To keep your porridge hot while you eat it, first warm your bowl. A bit of water in the bowl and 30 secs on HIGH in the micro does the warming trick. Or, use the milk you'd otherwise pour cold over the oatmeal as the liquid to warm your bowl.

Basil's Best Buttermilk Waffles

Young cooks tend to specialize in preparing the foods they really like. Basil simply loves waffles so he makes them for the family on weekends.

Gather together:
Waffle Maker – heat it up and brush it with oil/butter
1/2 t/2.5ml BS
1/2 t/2.5ml BP
1 T/15ml Icing Sugar
1 1/4 C/300ml Flour
2 Eggs, Yolks and Whites separated
2 C/480ml Buttermilk, well shaken
1 T/15ml Oil or melted Butter
Genuine Maple Syrup
Extra Butter (if you must)

Bowl # 1:
With a large whip mix together	BS, BP, sugar, flour.

Bowl # 2:
Whisk together	egg yolks buttermilk oil.

Bowl # 3:
In a metal bowl whisk until foamy	egg whites.

Combine the Bowls:
Gently mix bowl #2 into	bowl # 1.
Fold bowl #3 into	bowl # 1.

Pour into heated waffle maker:
Pour mixture into each section of the waffle maker, spreading out batter with a spatula to fill the sections

without excess (because excess batter will billow over the sides when the lid is closed!).
Keep waffles warm in an oven until serving time.
If you must, spread waffles with butter.
Pour over each waffle maple syrup.

TIP! To 'fold', run a rubber spatula down one side, across the bottom and up the other side, thus bringing the ingredients together without stirring. See diagram below.

2 Eggy Sandwiches
Here is a sweet and sour hot sandwich that satisfies many nutrient requirements for a good breakfast. Freeze #2!

Gather together:
1 very large or 2 large Eggs
3 T/45ml Milk
S & P
dash of Hot Sauce if desired
Grainy or other Mustard
Apricot Jam
4 slices Bread suitable for soaking up the egg mixture
2 slices Swiss Cheese
2 slices Ham
2 portions (4 deli slices) Sliced Chicken or Turkey
2 T/30ml Butter

Prepare custard and chutney mixes:
In a shallow bowl whisk lightly	eggs, milk, S & P hot sauce.
Mix together for chutney and spread it on	mustard and jam each slice of bread.

Put sandwiches together and cook:
On top of 2 bread slices place	cheese, ham, chicken or turkey.
Cover with 2 remaining	bread slices.
Heat in a large frypan	butter.
Dip a sandwich on both sides into	egg mixture.

Fry sandwiches in the hot butter to golden on each side, about 5 mins in all. Let stand a couple of mins before slicing into halves or thirds.
Make-a-Meal: Serve with sliced fruit or fruit salad with nuts.

Vegetables and Fruits

El.Wok/Frypan Recipes:	
Asparagus Spears for 1	26
Chinese Orange Broccoli for 4	28
Candied Carrots	29
Sweet Potato Hash Browns for 2	35
Orange Rice	36

Veggie and Fruit Tips	18
Flavour Enhancers and Aromatics	21
Apple and Sweet Potato Bake	25
Asparagus Spears for 1	26
Glazed Beets	27
Chinese Orange Broccoli for 4	28
Candied Carrots	29
Mary's Micro'd Corn-on-the-Cob	30
Micro'd Cukes and Peppers	31
Garlic Mashed Potatoes with Milk	32
Mediterranean Roasted Potatoes	33
Real Scalloped Potatoes for 1-2	34
Sweet Potato Hash Browns for 2	35
Orange Rice	36
Rice with Peas and Herbs	37
Sweet and Savoury Rice	38
Baked Tomatoes	40
Baked Veggies for the Gang	41
Baked Zucchini Boats for 2	42

VEGGIE AND FRUIT TIPS

Emphasis on Veggies and Fruits: Nutritionists and health professionals currently place huge emphasis on the positive effects of these foods. They tell us to fill a dinner plate three-quarters full with veggies and to eat at least 5 servings of them daily. Fruits are emphasized as ultra-healthy on the basis of their depth of colour, e.g., blueberries v bananas.

Storing Veggies & Fruits: All fresh produce with the exception of tomatoes, potatoes and globe onions keep best in the fridge. Always keep fruits and veggies stored in separate crispers – fruit gasses ruin veggies. Be sure the fruits and veggies are dry before placing them in plastic bags for storage.

Mushrooms keep well in a brown paper bag in the fridge.

Please, please, never refrigerate tomatoes as they will lose their flavour. **Bananas** may be kept in the fridge or at room temperature (the debate on that is ongoing).

Maintaining the Colour in Vegetables: Since we judge what we eat with our eyes as well as our taste buds, keeping the colour of our food looking 'fresh' after cooking really is important. In addition to looks, colour enhancers tend to bring balance to the veggie flavours, especially when they are strong like red beets.
For Green veggies, add a bit of SALT after the veggies heat up
For Red veggies, add ACID e.g. red wine vinegar
For White veggies, add MILK + LEMON JUICE
For Orange or Yellow veggies there is usually no need for colour enhancers.

Keeping 'Mush' Out of your Meal: Too many of us grew up in households where the veggies often turned to mush. That is absolutely not necessary! Nor is eating 'cooked' veggies practically raw. Just pay a little attention to your pot while a tender veg is cooking. Few take longer than about five mins if you are using the micro or a saucepan with a bit of liquid. (If you use a steamer, however, the cooking time may be double.) Longer cooking times are required for potatoes, rutabaga, beans, beets, large cut carrots and parsnips because these veggies have dense fibres.

Varieties of Apples: We are fortunate to have a wide variety of apples available all year round. Some are best for eating raw or in salads – Macintosh, Spartan, Gala. Others are good for baking – Granny Smith, Golden, Empire. The Northern Spy is the apple of choice for pie makers but it can be hard to find.

Varieties of Greens: What an explosion there has been in the kinds of greens we can choose from these days! Even local farmers are producing many more varieties than they did ten years ago. The best news about all the greens is that they taste terrific either cooked or raw and they possess tons of nutrients for your body's health. Try kale or rapine as well as spinach and broccoli. In the lettuce family, Romaine tops the raw nutrient list but all varieties contain good amounts of vitamins and minerals.

Varieties of Peppers:
There are several different sweet bell peppers and a host of chili peppers, each with its own nutritional and culinary uses. Commonly available <u>bell peppers</u> are green, red, orange and yellow. Eaten raw, bell peppers are high in nutrients.

Their nutrient score declines when the peppers are cooked but they are so colourful and useful that we cook them anyhow on the grill or in stir-fries. Chili peppers can be a mystery in terms of their heat quotient so they require experimentation. Western diets now incorporate them in their raw, dried and canned forms. Common to our palettes and usually available in supermarkets are mild yellow-green Cubanelles and hot dark green jalapeños, which in their smoked and canned form are known as chipotles. Be careful with thin red Serranos, tiny Thai or bird's eye chilis, and small round red Scotch Bonnets. They can knock off the roof of your mouth!

Frozen Orange Juice: Keep a can of frozen juice in the freezer and scoop out what you need for vinaigrette or whatever. The consistency of the frozen juice is always soft enough to scoop. Make a glass of juice this way too.

Fresh v Frozen fruits and vegetables: Nowadays, a huge variety of fruits and veggies can be found as fresh produce or in frozen packages. Each type is about equally nutritious. Obviously, fresh is best in summer and fall. But later and earlier in the year the better bang for your buck is often the frozen kind. Also, fresh fruits and veg that spend too long in the fridge lose much of their nutritional value.

Eggplant has the reputation of needing special handling before cooking, i.e., being salted and drained of excess bitter liquid. However, if you use small eggplants such as the little Japanese darlings, special prep is not required. Treat those just as you would zucchini slices or orbs of green tomato – slice and fry or bake, with or without a coating.

FLAVOUR ENHANCERS AND AROMATICS

Salt adds that extra 'oomph' that taste buds love. It is the most common flavour booster we use on an every day basis, at the table, in our cooking and especially in the prepared foods we buy. These days, many developed countries are attempting to re-educate their citizens about the dangers of excess salt in their diets. New daily percentage numbers have been issued for youngsters, teens, adults and oldsters and they are much lower than the amounts we've been used to.

The biggest salt culprits are grocery items including soup and take-away foods. Having said that, manufacturers are aware of the dangers of salt and many are working towards delivering tasty products with lower sodium. Also, fast-food emporiums have been posting the nutrition counts for each of their products and introducing more vegetable products with lower salt content.

While salt is a regular item in the recipes in this book it is really up to you to determine how much or how little you will include in the dish you are making. Some dishes obviously need/like salt: dishes containing oatmeal, corn and popcorn, pasta, the water for steaming lobster. And most baked goods require salt to complete the chemical changes from raw to cooked.

Apparently one's taste buds can adjust from too much salt to an acceptably lower level within about two weeks. If your blood pressure or your body weight is high, reducing salt in your everyday diet should be your #1 goal. But, please take note that some table salt that includes iodine is necessary to maintain body health!

Peppercorns: Various types and colours of peppercorns are on the grocery shelves. We are mostly familiar with black pepper that adds a pungent and sharp savoury taste. White pepper is used when you're making dishes that need a savoury kick but don't want little black specks. There are Asian 'peppercorns' too, some of which are not from the same plant but are used the same way as black or white peppercorns.

Spicy v Mild Chili Powders: In many grocery stores only a very few varieties of chili powders are available. Which one to buy? There are two main styles: ground chilies blended with other flavourings and single chili grinds.

The origin of the chili powder generally dictates its type and its spiciness. Chili powders from India and South Asian countries are usually very spicy since they are made from a single type of chili pepper. Many North American chili powders are the blended type, with flavours such as garlic and cumin added to fairly mild chilies. Some packaged powders indicate "hot" or "mild" on their labels.

Curry Powders These earthy/spicy/tangy/gentle/fiery powders and pastes have become staples in Western kitchens now that Asian and Indian powders and pastes are readily available in our grocery stores. Shopping for them in ethnic grocery stores both helps and hinders one's understanding of the many varieties because the labels are hard to decipher or understand. Thus, experimentation is the key to finding the curry powder you prefer, and for which dish.

Do not be afraid to mix a couple of different powders. For example, using one part Indian from a packet simply labeled "curry powder" and one part Asian curry powder or paste (garlic, red or green or yellow Thai, etc.) yields a reasonably sophisticated and spicy curry taste. Just be cautious and add small amounts to your dish, tasting as you go. The flavours in curry concoctions bloom with heat so go slow!

Taste, Flavours and Balance   Most people know what they like and dislike. But they may not realize the 'why' of their preferences. Of late, chefs and scientists have unraveled the origins and elements of taste. That information helps a cook to produce successful dishes.

Here are the five flavour categories:
Sour	as in lemon juice
Sweet	as in sugar
Salty	as in potato chips
Bitter	as in arugula
Umami	meaty/savoury as in soy sauce.

Accomplished chefs aim for dishes that balance these flavours so that the overall taste is not dominated by just one. Think fish with lemon sauce – the sauce must be subtly sour so that the gentle flavour of the fish shines through. (Grand Ma knows because she's made the mistake of adding way too much lemon juice and ruining the fish.)

Umami is a new flavour descriptor in the scientific world. Apparently it occurs in breast milk. Hence, mammals have a built-in affection for its flavour. Common foods that have high quotients of umami include tomatoes, cheeses, tuna, shrimp, prosciutto and the ubiquitous soy sauce.

Onions are a great flavour enhancer. They typically add sweetness to a dish but they can also seem too strong, even biting. One way to tame raw onions is to soak slices in ice water before using. Also, the ice bath reduces the onion's fumes, thus lessening the cook's tendency to sneeze or have watery eyes. Another popular flavour-taming method is to caramelize or slowly sauté slices until they turn golden or even dark brown. Several varieties of globe onions are always available, some sweeter and milder than others. Try Vidalias in the spring and red onions all year long. For many cooks, shallots (the small ones at bottom left) are always on hand as a 'go-to' onion for most recipes.

Apple and Sweet Potato Bake

Here is a mellow-tasting dish that goes well with ham and roasted pork.

Gather together:
2 Sweet Potatoes, peeled and cut into chunks
3 small Granny Smith Apples (this variety of apple keeps its shape), cut into chunks the same size as the sweet potatoes and not peeled
1/3 C/**80ml** Brown Sugar mixed with 1/2 t/**2.5ml** Salt and **scant** 1/4 t/**1.25ml** ground Allspice
2 T/**30ml** Butter cut into bits
1/4 C/**60ml** Water (potato cooking water + extra)

Create layers:
Cook until just tender, about 15 mins and then drain off the water into a jug. the sweet potatoes
Into a greased casserole, using half of each ingredient, put equal layers of potatoes
apples
and sprinkle with half the sugar/salt/allspice.
Over a second layer of apples
scatter butter bits.
Then make a second layer of potatoes/allspice/sugar/salt.

Add the reserved water.
Cover with foil.
Bake at 350F/180C:
for 30 mins.
Uncover casserole and bake another 15 mins to brown the top.

Asparagus Spears for 1
STOVE/EL.WOK/FRYPAN

These days, good quality fresh asparagus is available year round. But it is always better in the spring when fat, sweet spears tempt the winter-weary palate. Here is a recipe for perfect steamed asparagus that can be done in a wok or pot.

Gather together:
6-8 spears glossy green Asparagus Spears
1/2 C/**120ml** Water
pinch Salt
1 t/**5ml** Butter
2-3 grinds Black Pepper
1 fresh Lemon wedge

Rack, steam, garnish:
Using a pan (or el.wok/frypan) as wide as the spears build a 'trivet/rack' of asparagus with 3-4 on bottom and 3-4 angled on top.
Add water.
Quickly bring water to the boil
and sprinkle spears all over with salt.
Cover, turn heat down to low and steam about 3 mins, until spears are **almost** fork tender.
Turn off heat.
Drain off water and return asparagus to pot and to hot element or return cooked spears to the still warm el.wok/frypan.
Add butter
and shake pan/el.wok/frypan.
Squeeze lemon juice
over asparagus and butter.
Serve immediately.

Glazed Beets

For this exceptionally sweet and tasty dish use canned beets or fresh beets that you have roasted. See **"TIP!"** below.

Gather together:
Oil
1 can sliced Beets/ **4 fresh** Beets roasted, skinned, sliced
1-2 t/**5-10ml** Lemon zest
3 T/**45ml** Lemon juice
1/2 t/**2.5ml** Salt, preferably Kosher or Sea
1/2 C/**120ml** liquid Honey (melt grainy honey in the micro!)
2 T/**30ml** Butter cut into bits

Put the ingredients together:
Brush a shallow baking dish with   oil.
In one layer arrange   beet slices.
Sprinkle with   lemon zest & juice
    salt.

Pour over all   honey.
Dot with   butter bits.
Cover with foil.
Bake at 350/180C:
for 15-20 mins until beets are well glazed.

TIP! Roasted fresh beets have a sweet and earthy taste that bears no relationship to canned beets. To roast them, spread a large sheet of foil over a baking pan. Lay on the whole washed beets and sprinkle them all over with oil. Gather up the foil to make a package. Roast about one hour at 350F/180C, until beets are tender. Cool a bit before slipping off their skins, starting with a knife cut at the root end. Cut each beet in half. Place the flat side on a cutting board and slice into 1/4"/0.6cm pieces.

Chinese Orange Broccoli for 4   SKILLET/ EL.WOK/FRYPAN

Sometimes a kicked-up veg makes a meal special. This broccoli recipe will certainly do the trick.

Gather together:
splash of Vegetable Oil
head of fresh Broccoli, separated into flowerets
2 large cloves Garlic, minced
1 T/**15ml** minced Gingerroot
2 T/**30ml** Soy Sauce
dash of Water
1 t/**5ml** Sesame Oil
1 T/**15ml** Orange Marmalade
1 Orange, Zest and peeled Sections

Flame up the Skillet/Wok/Frypan:

On med heat, add to your pan	oil.
When oil is hot add and stir 2 mins	broccoli.
Stir in	garlic, gingerroot, soy sauce.
Add	a dash of water.
Cover pan and cook 2 mins.	
Uncover and stir in	sesame oil marmalade.
Add and stir to just heat up	orange zest and sections.

Serve with hot rice to soak up the juices.

TIP! Keep gingerroot wrapped in paper towels in your crisper. To peel its delicate skin, use the tip of a spoon or a peeler.

Candied Carrots
STOVE/ EL.WOK/FRYPAN

To dress up an ordinary dinner plate use this recipe. It's quick and easy too. You may substitute squashes or parsnips for carrots. Candied veggies go well with meats and sausages.

Gather together:
1 small pkg julienned Carrots
Salted Water
1/2 C/**120ml** Melted Butter
1/2 C/**120ml** Brown Sugar
1/4 t/**1.25ml** Ground Allspice

Cook and Glaze the carrots:
In large saucepan with lid/el. wok/frypan
boil salted water.
Add carrots.
Cook, covered, on med-low heat to crisp-tender stage, about 4 mins.
Drain carrots and return them to pan.
Pour over carrots and stir well melted butter
sugar
allspice.
Cover pot loosely* and cook on <u>low</u> about 8-10 mins, stirring occasionally to glaze.

TIP! Carrots keep well in the crisper, wrapped in a plastic bag. But do not store them near apples because the gas emitted from apples causes carrots to taste bitter.

*TIP! Covering a pot loosely means that the lid sits askew the top of the pot so any steam escapes instead of cooking the ingredients further (and ruining their texture).

Mary's Micro'd Corn-on-the-Cob　　　　　　　MICRO
Preparing corn this way could not be faster or tastier!

Gather together:
dash of Oil or **dab** of Butter
1 or 2 fresh cobs of Corn, husks left on

Prepare and cook the corn:
Leave the husk on the　　　　　　　corn cob
but slice a circle through the husk
almost at the base of the cob (to allow
for easy husk removal after cooking).
Microwave 2 mins on HIGH　　　　　corn cob.
Allow cooked corn to sit before
husking because of steam inside.

Micro'd Cukes and Peppers

Use your microwave to 'stir-fry' veggies of the same type and size, such as peppers and cukes or a variety of summer squashes cut into cubes.

Gather together:
1 T/**15ml** Butter or Oil
1 T/**15ml** chopped Onion
1 clove Garlic, crushed
1/2 Red Pepper cut into pieces
1/4 Cuke, peeled and cut into pieces
1 t/**5ml** Lemon Juice

Micro 1-2-3:
Into a micro bowl put   butter or oil
                                             onion
                                               garlic.

Micro on HIGH 1 min.
Stir.
Add to the bowl   red pepper pieces
                                               cukes.

Micro on HIGH 1 min.
Stir.
Micro on HIGH 30 secs.
Test for doneness.
Sprinkle over all   lemon juice.
Eat!

Garlic Mashed Potatoes with Milk   MICRO

Because the garlic cloves are cooked, their flavour is soft and muted, not sharp. The amounts in this recipe make at least 2 servings. Keep leftovers in a covered container in the fridge and reheat in the micro or fry gently in a skillet/el.wok/frypan.

Gather together:
4 cloves Garlic
2 large Potatoes
Water
Salt
1-2 T/**15-30ml** Butter, softened
1/2 C/**120ml** Milk

Cook:
Peel and cut into quarters/ eighths	potatoes.
Smash and remove skins of	garlic cloves.
Add potatoes and garlic to a	microwave safe dish
with a bit of	water and salt.

Micro the potatoes according to your micro's instructions, until fully cooked.

Mash, micro and add :
Use a metal masher or ricer to mash	cooked potatoes.
With a wooden spoon beat in	butter.
Micro on HIGH for 30-45 secs	milk
and, using a wooden spoon, beat into mashed potatoes	hot milk.
Add to your taste	S & P.

Reheat in the microwave if necessary at serving time.

Mediterranean Roasted Potatoes for 1
For 2 portions, just double the ingredients.

Gather together:
1 Potato, preferably unpeeled, cut into 4 pieces
1 t/**5ml** Olive Oil
1/4 t/**1.25ml** dried Rosemary **or** 1- 2 t/**5-10ml** fresh chopped Rosemary (be careful, rosemary has a strong flavor)
1/2 t /**2.5ml** grated Lemon Zest (use a hardware store rasp)
S & P
squeeze of fresh Lemon Juice
or dash of Balsamic Vinegar

Prepare potatoes on a foil-lined baking tray:
Mix together	oil, rosemary, lemon zest.
Add and mix to coat pieces	potato.
Sprinkle with	S & P.

Roast potatoes at 400F/200C:
30-40 mins in an oven or toaster oven, turning once.

Sprinkle roasted potatoes with	lemon juice or balsamic.

Make-a-meal: Sautéd or grilled proteins along with colourful grilled veggies allow the fresh but earthy flavour of the potatoes to shine.

TIP! Heart-healthy olive oils are sold under several labels. The most common in North America are extra-virgin, virgin and cold pressed. The first two grades are the healthiest since the olives have been pressed without heat or chemicals. Kept in a cool, dark spot, olive oils last and taste fresh for about a year.

Real Scalloped Potatoes for 1-2

Preparing a dish of real scalloped potatoes for one or two servings takes prep time of about 10 mins. So why buy expensive deli potatoes or poor nutrition packages?

Gather together:
1 T/**15ml** + 1 t/**5ml** soft Butter
1 or 2 medium Potatoes, sliced 1/8 to 1/4"/**.3-.6cm** thick
1/2 small Onion, thinly sliced
1 1/2 T/**22ml** Flour, divided in 2 halves
S & P
pinch of Nutmeg
Milk or Cream, about 1/2 C/**120ml**
Tinfoil

Half fill a small baking dish:
Brush your baking dish with   1 t/**5ml** butter.
Place in the dish <u>one half</u> of   potato slices.
Top with a few slices of   onion.
Sprinkle with <u>half</u> the   flour.
Sprinkle with <u>half</u> the   S & P and nutmeg.
Dot with tiny bits of the   1 T/ of **15ml** butter.
Repeat the layers and finish the dish:
Into the sides of the dish pour   milk or cream
just to cover the top of the ingredients.
Cover, bake, uncover and bake again:
Cover the dish with   tinfoil.
Bake at 350F/180C:
for 40 mins until
potatoes are very tender.
Uncover the dish.
Return it to the oven for 10 mins
or so, until the top is golden.

Sweet Potato Hash Browns for 2   SKILLET/ EL.WOK/FRYPAN

Sometimes all you need to jazz up an ordinary meal is something a little different. Here it is.

Gather together:
1 small White Potato
1/2 medium Sweet Potato (rub cut side of left-over sweet potato with lemon, wrap in plastic and refrigerate)
1/2 t/**2.5ml** dried Sage leaves, crumbled
1 Egg, beaten
1 T/**15ml** Flour
2 strips Bacon, cooked and chopped
S & P
1 1/2 T/**22ml** Oil

Grate the potatoes:
Using a large-hole grater, grate   white and sweet potatoes.

Add to potatoes and stir together   sage, egg, flour, bacon, S & P.

Make the hash into a potato cake:
In an 8"/**20cm** skillet or el.wok/frypan
heat on med-low   oil.
Transfer potato mixture to pan
and press potatoes to flatten into a cake.
Cook about 10 mins until bottom browns.
Slip a wide spatula under the cake
and slide it out onto a plate, then
flip the cake back into the pan
with the uncooked side down.
Cook about 5 mins more to brown bottom.

Orange Rice
SKILLET/ EL.WOK/FRYPAN

Here is a foolproof method for cooking rice. The addition of citrus takes ordinary rice to a new and delightful level of taste.

Gather together:
1/2 C/**120ml** Long grain Rice
1/2 C/**120ml** Orange Juice topped up with Water to make **total liquid** of 1 C/**240ml** (twice as much liquid as rice)
1/2 t/**2.5ml** Salt
1 large Orange for 1 T/**15ml** grated Zest

Prepare the Rice:
In a small pot with lid/el.wok/frypan put   rice
    orange juice
    & water
    salt.

Stir these ingredients together.
Cook the rice:
Bring pot/wok/frypan to a boil, uncovered.
Turn heat down to simmer or lowest heat level.
Stir again and cover pot/wok/frypan.
Leave without peeking for 20 mins.
Uncover pot.
Sprinkle over cooked rice   orange zest.
Fluff rice gently with a fork.

TIP! Zesting is a breeze if you use a rasp in one hand and hold and roll the fruit around in the other hand so that each swipe of the rasp grates a different section of the fruit's rind, leaving the white pith behind on the fruit.

Rice with Peas and Herbs   MICRO

This recipe makes an almost instant rice dish that can accompany a protein or, with shredded protein added, makes an almost complete meal in one dish.

Gather together:
2 servings Cooked Rice, about 1 1/4 C/**300ml**
2 T/**30ml** Orange Juice
1 handful Currants
1 T/**15ml** chopped Fresh Dill or Mint
S & P if desired
1 handful shredded Protein if desired (chicken, ham, salmon)
1/2 C/**120ml** frozen Peas

1: 2: 3: 4:
In a micro dish combine all ingredients.
Micro on HIGH 2 mins.
Stir gently.
Check for desired temp.
Serve!

Make-a-Meal: All you need to add is a crunchy salad.

TIP! Many cooks automatically use long grain white rice for side dishes. But brown rice is considerably more nutritious, has less natural sodium than its white sister and is not at all difficult to cook. Buy some and cook according to package directions.

TIP! Keep cooked rice in the fridge for several days and use left overs in soups and salads.

Sweet & Savoury Rice

A combination of rice with other ingredients is often known as a pilaf. In this recipe, sweet dried apricots, currants and dried cranberries contrast with savoury onion, garlic and herbs. The quantities below make plenty for 3 servings. Left overs can be frozen.

Gather together:
1 C/**240ml** rinsed Rice, long grain white or brown
1 C/**240ml** Water **+** 1 C/**240ml** Chicken Stock
 (+ additional 1/2 C/**120ml** liquid if using brown rice)
2 T/**30ml** melted Butter **+** 1 T/**15ml** Butter & 1 T/**15ml** Oil for frying
1 Red Onion, sliced thin
1 t/**5ml** minced Garlic
1 C/**240ml** chopped Dried Fruits – apricots, currants, cranberries – or other dried fruits of your choice such as dates, figs, cherries
1-2 T/**15-30ml** minced Herbs such as parsley, chives, green onion

Cook the rice:

In a 2L pot with lid bring to boil	water & stock.
Stir in	rinsed rice.

Turn heat to simmer, cover pot and let cook 20-30 mins.
Remove lid and fluff with a fork to test for doneness. (Brown rice takes longer to cook and uses more liquid than white rice.)
If liquid remains, drain rice and let it sit while veggies cook.

Sauté vegetables:
Heat a large frypan with   butter & oil.
When sizzling, add   onion, garlic
and turn heat down to cook
and soften veggies.
Add and stir in   dried fruits.
Gently stir in   cooked rice, herbs.
Warm the mixture about 5 mins
on low heat.

Make-a-meal: Any simply cooked fish or meat will be lovely with the pilaf. Add a green salad and you'll have a delicious and nutritious feast!

Baked Tomatoes OVEN/TOASTER OVEN

This tomato dish makes a colourful and tasty addition to a grilled meat meal. Your toaster oven is a good appliance for this recipe. For a company meal, multiply the ingredients by 2 or 3 and use your large oven.

Gather together:
2 ripe but firm Tomatoes, halved cross-wise
2 T/**30ml** fine Bread Crumbs
1 t/**5ml** dry grated Cheese such as Parmesan OR
1 T/**15ml** shredded semi-hard Cheese such as cheddar
1 clove Garlic, minced
1/2 t/**2.5ml** dried Thyme
pinch Sugar
S & P
Butter or Oil for greasing the pan
1 T/**15ml** fresh Basil, chopped

Mix up the crumbs:
Using your fingers mix together the bread crumbs, cheese, garlic, thyme, sugar.

Prepare the tomatoes for baking:
Sprinkle the tomato halves with S & P.
Pat on top of each half bread crumb mixture.

Grease a foil-lined baking tray with butter/oil
and place tomatoes on it, sprinkling
tomatoes and crumbs with basil.
Bake at 375F/190C:
about 20 mins until crumbs are golden and tomatoes are hot.

Baked Veggies for the Gang

Here is a method that produces well flavoured, tender and golden vegetables roasted/baked in the oven. Delicious with any roasted meat or salmon. The amounts below are plenty for 4 servings. For more, just multiply the ingredients.

Gather together:
4 small Red and White skin Potatoes, quartered, unpeeled
2 Carrots, peeled, cut in 1"/**2.5cm** chunks
1 medium Onion, cut into **4** wedges through the roots to keep wedges whole
4 cloves Garlic, smashed
1/4 C/**60ml** Balsamic Vinegar
1/4 C/**60ml** melted Butter
1 T/**15ml** fresh Thyme, chopped or 1 t/**5ml** dried Thyme
1 t/**5ml** S
1/2 t/**2.5ml** P
Special equipment: rimmed baking sheet, tinfoil

Lay out the veggies:
Line a rimmed baking sheet with foil
and lay out in single layer   all the veggies.
Season the veggies:
In a measuring cup combine   balsamic vinegar
                                       melted butter
                                       thyme
                                       S & P.
Drizzle over the veggies and toss to coat.
Cover the pan with more foil.
Roast at 425F/220C:
for 45 mins, shaking pan occasionally.
Remove foil to finish cooking and
browning, another 15 mins or so,
until veggies are tender and golden.

Baked Zucchini Boats for 2 – a method recipe

If you grow zucchini, or if the zucchini fairy visits you, why not make boats out of the first growth (the small ones or the even smaller fingerlings)? Veggie boats are showy and tasty and simple to create. They pair nicely with sausage or chicken that can be baked in the same oven for about the same time. This method may be applied to squashes, bell peppers and fingerling potatoes (with adjustments to baking times.)

Gather together:
2 small or 4 fingerling Zucchini
1 clove Garlic, minced finely
1 T/**15ml** finely minced Onion
2 slices Tomato, diced small
1 t/**5ml** dried or 1 T/**15ml** fresh Basil, chopped
S & P
1-2 T/**15-30ml** grated Parmesan or Cheddar Cheese

Slice, scoop, mix, pat, sprinkle:
Slice in half lengthwise   small zucchini
and scoop out half the flesh or,
for fingerlings, take a thin top slice
and then scoop out the flesh.
Mix with the zucchini flesh the   garlic, onion, tomato, basil, S & P.

Pat mixture into each zucchini boat.
Sprinkle boats with   cheese.
Bake the boats at 350F/180C:
on a tinfoil tray, about 30 mins in an
oven or toaster oven until the filling
is hot and the boats are tender.

Salads, Sauces and Soups

Lobster & Avocado Cocktail	44
Condiment Fixer-Uppers	45
Blue Cheese Iceberg Wedges	46
Your Own Vinaigrette	47
Carrot Salad or Slaw	48
Chicken Caesar Salad for 1 +	49
Good Things Salad	50
Tomato Salad for 2	51
Anne's Waldorf Salad	52
Crunchy Whole Meal Salad for 1	53
Cheese Sauce	54
Your Own Gravy/Sauce	55
Anne's Quick Tomato Sauce	56
Mixed Bean Soup	58
Old-style Onion Soup for 2	59
Hearty Pea and Sausage Soup	60
Soups & Stews Dumplings	62

Lobster & Avocado Cocktail

When you want a dazzling starter for a special meal this is it. The best taste comes from freshly steamed lobster but frozen lobster tails or frozen canned lobster meat works too. This recipe makes 2 large or 4 small servings.

Gather together:
1 1/2 C/**360ml** Lobster Meat cut into cubes
1 large or 2 small Avocados, cubed or sliced, sprinkled with lemon juice (to prevent browning)
1/2 C/**120ml** shredded Lettuce
1/4 C/**80ml** or more Cocktail Sauce
2 dashes Worcestershire Sauce
dashes of Hot Sauce to taste
Lemon or Lime **wedges** for garnish

Mix together all ingredients **except**	lobster and avocado.
Taste for consistency – perhaps add	more cocktail sauce.
Taste for flavour – perhaps add more	Worcestershire /lemon juice/ hot sauce.

Then...
Gently stir in	lobster.

Make a beautiful presentation in stemmed glasses:
Place in glasses	a few avocado pieces.
Cover with one serving of	lobster with sauce.
Cover with	remaining avocado.
Garnish with	lemon or lime.

TIP! If you use frozen and canned lobster, make sure to rinse and drain the meat well. Also, pick through the meat to remove any bits of cartilage.

Condiment Fixer-Uppers
Sometimes all you need to spice up a meal is a dressing or a condiment that is just a little different.

Warm & Tangy Dressing for Greens and Veggies:
Warm up 1-2 T/**15-30ml** Marmalade in the microwave. Whisk together 2 T/**30ml** Wine Vinegar and 1/3 C/**80ml** good Olive Oil. Add to the oil and vinegar 1t/**5ml** Poppy or Sesame Seeds and a **pinch** of S & P and combine with the warm marmalade.

Cranberry-Marmalade Jam for Meats and Poultry:
Process or stir together equal parts of Cranberry Sauce and Marmalade.

Spicy Jelled Topping for Brie/Camembert with Crackers:
Stir together **equal amounts** of red currant jelly or firm cranberry sauce with a **bit** of grainy mustard;
OR
Melt the jelly in the micro for 30-45 secs and then stir in 1 t/**5ml** Balsamic vinegar. Allow jelly to jell again.

Roasted Meat Red Currant Sauce:
Into the pan juices from roasted meat, after juices have been brought to a boil, stir in at least 1 T/**15ml** Red Currant Jelly and simmer to thicken. If desired, add a **strip** of orange peel while the sauce thickens. If the sauce needs to be thinned, squeeze in **some** juice from the orange. Taste and season with S & P.

Blue Cheese Iceberg Wedges

A salad of Iceberg lettuce wedges with blue cheese dressing was popular fifty years ago and now it's back on restaurant menus. This dressing was developed by super chef Bobby Flay and adapted by Anne.

Gather together:
1/2 C/**120ml** (genuine) Mayonnaise
1/3 C/**80ml** Sour Cream
1-2 t/**5-10ml** Dijon Mustard
1/4 C/**60ml** Crumbled Blue Cheese
2 T/**30ml** fresh Lemon Juice
S & freshly ground Pepper
1/4 C/**60ml** White Wine if desired for thinning the sauce
Optional: **dash or 2** of Hot Sauce for zing
Crisp Iceberg Lettuce, cut into **large chunks or wedges**
Optional garnishes: chopped Tomatoes, Chives, Jalapeños

Toss all ingredients together:	except lettuce
Spoon dressing over:	lettuce wedges.
If desired, garnish with	tomatoes, chives, jalapeños.

TIP! The flavours of blue cheese and grilled chicken or beef go well together. So be sure to serve this salad <u>with</u> your meal.

TIP! Blue cheese keeps a long time in your fridge provided it is well wrapped to keep moisture and aroma in the cheese, not out in your fridge. So your own blue cheese dressing is economical as well as tastier than bottled dressing.

TIP! Crisp lettuce ahead of time by soaking it in **warm** water, draining it on a towel, then storing in the fridge in a plastic bag.

Your Own Vinaigrette
There is nothing like your own dressing to make a green salad taste like you are dining in France! Use sherry vinegar if you can afford it. Enough for 8 salad servings. (Be sure to dress the greens lightly)

Gather together
4 t/**20ml** Sherry or white wine Vinegar
1 Shallot, finely minced
1/2 t/**2.5ml** Dijon Mustard
1/2 t/**2.5ml** or less Sea Salt
1/4 t/**1.25ml** Freshly ground Black Pepper
1/4 C/**60ml** Extra-virgin Olive Oil (EVOO)
Optional: **1/4** fresh Lemon, juice squeezed in

Shake it up:
Whisk in a jar with a good lid   all ingredients.
Shake the dressing vigorously!
Taste and add if desired   squeeze of lemon.

Carrot Salad or Slaw

Simple. Colourful. Tasty. The amounts below serve 2-4 as part of a main plate. Don't be shy about varying the amounts or adding other ingredients such as shredded bell peppers.

Gather together:
1/2 small can Pineapple Bits, shredded, well drained
1 C/**240ml** shredded Carrots or bagged matchstick carrots
1 large handful Raisins
1/4 C/**60ml** Sugar
1/4 t/**1.25ml** crushed Red Pepper Flakes
1/2 C/**120ml** Mayonnaise
S & P
1 T/**15ml** chopped Chives

Combine the ingredients:
In a bowl combine	pineapple
	carrots
	raisins.
Sprinkle over top	sugar
	red pepper flakes.
Mix in well	mayo.
Refrigerate 1 hour to meld flavours.	
Taste and possibly add	salt and pepper.
Sprinkle over the slaw when serving:	chives.

TIP! For a beautiful presentation, line a bowl with lettuce leaves and mound the salad inside the lettuce.

TIP! Additional good things you may add to this salad are mango bits, thinly sliced celery and salted peanuts or cashews.

Chicken Caesar Salad for 1 +

This is a useful and nutritious recipe for a large lunch or small supper. You may add other colourful vegetables such as cooked green peas, celery slices, tomato wedges, carrot slices and you may multiply the amounts to make additional servings.

Gather together:
1/3 C/**80ml** BBQ Chicken, cubed, without skin
(or more if you're really hungry)
1/3 C to 1/2 C/**80-120ml** cubed coloured Sweet Peppers
small handful of bite-sized pieces of Romaine or other sturdy Lettuce
about 1/2 t/**2.5ml +/-** Garlic, minced, for 1 serving
1-3 T/**15-45ml** Store-bought Creamy Caesar Dressing
1/2 Lemon
1 T/**15ml** Parmesan Cheese
2 T/**30ml** Croutons if you wish

Prepare the Salad:
Toss together   chicken
                                                       peppers
                                                       lettuce
                                                       garlic.

Dress the Salad:
Toss salad again with   dressing.
Squeeze over the salad   lemon half.
Sprinkle over salad   Parmesan cheese.
Top salad with   croutons if desired.

TIP! You might prefer to eat this salad with a crusty roll instead of using croutons. There is no need for further seasoning such as S & P because of all the seasoning in the chicken and the robust flavours of the cheese and lemon and dressing.

Good Things Salad for 1
So simple! So good! So good for you!

<u>Gather together:</u>
1/4 C/**60ml** Fresh sliced Strawberries
1/4 C/**60ml** Fresh Blueberries
1/2 T/**8ml** Slivered Almonds (keep almonds in a zip-lock bag in your freezer)
1 T/**15ml** Dried Cranberries
handful of Greens, washed and dried and crisped
about 1 T/**15ml** Ranch/Poppy Seed Dressing
2 T/**30ml** Feta cheese, crumbled

<u>and then:</u>

Put together in a bowl	all ingredients <u>except</u> dressing and feta.
Fold through the salad	the dressing.
Sprinkle the salad with	the feta.

TIP! If you can get to a bulk store, you'll find the prices of nuts and dried fruits much better than in a grocery store. But only buy bulk if you can use up the products.

TIP! Try to always keep some greens in your crisper. Here's how to clean and keep them...Fill up your clean kitchen sink with warm or cold water (it's a debate!). Dump in the greens and swish them around to release bits of dirt (which will fall to the bottom of your sink). Scoop up the greens and dry them in a salad spinner OR put them into a clean towel, scrunch up the ends in your fist and swing the towel around. Water will come flying out! Store the dry greens in a large zip bag in your fridge for several days. They're all ready to go when you need them.

Tomato Salad for 2
August is the best month for tomato salads since the sugars in locally grown tomatoes have developed by then. But now we can buy decent tasting tomatoes all year round. Try them!

Gather together:
1/2 C/**120ml** Balsamic Vinegar
1 t/**5ml** Capers, chopped
4 Basil Leaves, sliced
4 Olives, sliced
2 Anchovies, minced (do not be afraid!)
2 fresh, juicy Tomatoes, sliced or quartered
4 Lettuce leaves

Make the dressing:
Place in a large cup in the micro   balsamic vinegar
and boil on HIGH to reduce and
thicken, stirring occasionally,
for three 30 second cooking periods.
Add one more 30 secs to thicken more.
Cool the vinegar.

Mix gently together for the Salad: capers
basil
olives
anchovies
fresh tomatoes.

Finish the salad:
Place lettuce leaves on a plate or
shallow bowl and top with tomato mixture.
Drizzle reduced balsamic over salad.

Make-a-meal: This salad will be terrific with grilled or baked meats, fish, baked beans, or eggs on toast.

Anne's Waldorf Salad

This amount serves two as a dinner accompaniment. Everyone loves it! Especially good with pork.

Gather together:
2 heaping **T/30+ml** genuine Mayonnaise
1 heaping **T/15+ml** Frozen Orange Juice, not diluted
small handful of Raisins, any kind
1 large crisp Apple
1 small rib Celery
small handful of Grapes, seedless
Optional: 1 T/**15ml** Walnut or Almond pieces, toasted for about 5 mins at 300F/150C

Optional additions to the dressing:
   1 t/**5ml** Dijon Mustard
   1 t/**5ml** Curry powder
   1 t/**5ml** Orange or Lemon zest

Prepare the Salad Dressing:
Into a small bowl stir together
   mayo
   orange juice
   raisins.

Cover and refrigerate until needed. Making the dressing in advance plumps up the raisins.

Make the Salad:
Into the salad bowl slice/dice
   apple with skin
   celery
   grapes.

Blend in the dressing.
Refrigerate until served.
If using, add at serving time
   toasted nuts.

Crunchy Whole Meal Salad for 1
Broccoli or cauliflower binds with the cheese that dresses up this nutritious and delicious salad.

Gather together:
1 T/**15ml** plain Yogurt
1 T/**15ml** Mayonnaise
1 t/**5ml** fresh Lemon Juice
S & P
dash of Paprika
1/3-1/2 C/**100ml** Broccoli or Cauliflower flowerets*
2 slices red Onion, separated into rings
4 cherry Tomatoes, halved
1-2 T/**15-30ml** shredded or grated Cheddar Cheese
1/3 C/**80ml** bite-sized pieces Cooked Chicken
* If you prefer your broccoli and cauliflower to be tender, not crunchy, blanch the flowerets in boiling water with a bit of salt for about two mins; then dump the flowerets into ice water to stop the cooking; then drain well.

Make the Dressing:
Whisk together	yogurt, mayo, lemon juice, S & P, paprika.

Taste! Adjust seasonings if needed.
Put the salad ingredients together:
Combine in serving bowl	broccoli or cauliflower, all remaining ingredients.
Gently stir and toss salad with	dressing.

Let the salad sit for 30 mins to meld the flavours.

Cheese Sauce

Here is a basic cheese sauce for veggies and savoury supper dishes such as omelets, meat loaf and fish cakes.

Gather together:
3 T/**45ml** Butter
3 T/**45ml** Flour
1 1/2 C/**360ml** Milk
S & P
1/2 to 1 C/**120-240ml** grated Cheese, cheddar for example
pinch Dry Mustard if desired

Cook on the stovetop:
In a small pan on med-low heat melt	butter.
Stir in and cook stirring 2 mins*	flour.
Whisk in slowly	milk.
Season with	S & P.
Cook, stirring, until sauce thickens.	
Add and stir to melt	cheese.
Add, if using	mustard.

Taste for seasoning and add more cheese and mustard if desired or more milk if sauce is too thick.

TIP! Keep sauce warm over simmering water using a film of plastic wrap placed directly on the cooked sauce. That prevents a scum from forming on the top of the sauce.

***TIP!** By cooking butter and flour together for a couple of minutes, your sauce loses the floury taste that will ruin the taste of the dishes beneath the sauce.

Your Own Gravy/Sauce
If you have liquid in the pan after your meat or fowl is roasted, it is a snap to make a gravy/sauce to complete the dish.

Gather together:
about 2 T/**30ml** Drippings from the cooked roast resting platter
1 C+/**240+ml** of liquid poured from roasting pan, spooning off melted fat from the top and adding broth (or water) if necessary
1/4 C/**60ml** Wine or Broth, red/white/chicken/beef/veg
2-3 T/**30-45ml** Instant Flour
S & P
1 T/**15ml** soft Butter

After the meat or fowl is cooked and is resting:
Place roasting pan on med heat with	drippings.
Add and stir up brown bits with the	wine/broth.
Stir in and cook 2 mins	flour.
Add and stir in the cup of	liquid
and boil to 1/2 volume (1/2 C/**120ml**).	
Taste before adding	S & P.
Swirl in for a satiny finish	butter.
Add more liquid if gravy is too thick.	

Your Own Turkey Gravy.
The secret to a rich turkey gravy is a good broth. Prepare that in advance of turkey day by roasting turkey wing/neck bones (buy these separately), along with a roughly chopped carrot, a celery rib, an onion (cut into quarters but not peeled) and a garlic clove, for about an hour at 350F/180C, until bones are very brown. Then add water and wine/broth, about 3 cups/**720ml**, and stir up all the brown bits. Return the pan to the oven for 1/2 hour until the stock is a rich brown. Strain off liquid, pressing on solids. Add S & P to taste. Refrigerate.

Anne's Quick Tomato Sauce

When you crave a tomato pasta supper but don't have store-bought marinara (made with tomatoes, garlic, onions, herbs) sauce on hand, simmer up this tasty version in half an hour.

Gather together:
1/2 C/**120ml** canned Tomatoes with a little juice
2 T/**30ml** Tomato Paste
1 T/**15ml** Oil
1/3 C/**80ml** diced Onion
2 cloves Garlic, minced or simply smashed
1/2 Bay Leaf, crumbled
1/2 t/**2.5ml** Red Pepper flakes (or more)
1/4 t/**1.25ml** Sugar
Garnish: grated Parmesan Cheese
Optional: **1/2** Carrot, diced very small; **1/4** Red Pepper, diced; 1T/**15ml** chopped fresh Basil, **a few** Chili Flakes to taste

Put the veggies in the pot:
Heat in a heavy pot on med-low	oil.
Add and sweat for about 5 mins stirring occasionally.	onions
Stir in but do not brown	garlic.
Throw in	remaining ingredients

except basil and chili flakes.
Stir in and break up the (You may add more juice from the can or a little water if the sauce seems too thick.)	tomatoes.

Bring the sauce to a boil,
then turn down the heat to low
and let the sauce reduce and

thicken for about 20 mins.
If the sauce still seems too thick
add a bit of   <u>pasta water/water.</u>
Taste for seasoning and maybe add   chili flakes.
Add, if needed   S & P.
**But do not forget that tinned tomatoes
already contain plenty of salt.**
If you are using it, stir in at the end   fresh basil.
<u>Serve and Garnish:</u>
Add to the sauce   your cooked pasta
and swirl it around to coat each
strand with sauce before serving.
Garnish the sauce with   Parmesan.

TIP! You may cook pasta in an electric wok/frypan, bringing to the boil almost as much water as your pan will hold. Add salt. Stir in 1/2 cup/**120ml** of pasta (which yields the same amount of cooked pasta). While the pasta cooks, stir occasionally to allow each piece of pasta to heat, soften and cook through.

Mixed Bean Soup

In about 20 mins you can have a steaming bowl of delicious soup for yourself, with left overs to freeze.

Gather together:
1 T/**15ml** Olive Oil
1 Onion, finely chopped
3 cloves Garlic, smashed and cut up
2 small or 1 large can Mixed Beans, rinsed
1.75L good quality low-sodium Broth – veal, beef, chicken, vegetable
1/2 C/**120ml** small Pasta such as macaroni, orzo, broken spaghettini, etc.
1 t/**5ml** dried Tarragon

Add and cook and stir:
In a large saucepan heat on med-low	oil.
Add and cook 5 mins to soften	onion pieces.
Add and cook, stirring, 1 min	garlic.
Add, stir well, cover, bring to boil	beans
	broth.
Add in and stir well	pasta.
Cook pasta to the 'al dente' stage, usually about 7 mins. (see pkg directions)	
Stir in	tarragon.
Taste. If needed, add	S & P.

Make a meal: Serve this soup with hearty bread and a bit of cheese. You might grate the cheese on top of the bread and toast the cheesy bread in the toaster oven.

Old-style Onion Soup for 2
The flavour of this wonderfully warming soup is hard to beat. It makes a great lunch or supper on its own when a crouton and cheese are floated on top.

Gather together:
1 T/15ml Butter
2 large sweet Onions, sliced as thinly as you can
1 clove Garlic, smashed but not minced
1/4 t/1.25ml each dried Rosemary & dried Thyme, chopped
1 C/240ml Chicken Stock, low sodium if possible
S & White Pepper
Parsley for garnish
Optional: **a large** Crouton or toasted baguette slice
1/4 C/60ml Shredded Swiss or meltable Cheese

Sweat, sweat, sweat:
In a heavy saucepan with lid heat	butter.
Add and stir to sweat on med heat	onions
	garlic
	rosemary.

On low heat, cover pot and continue to stir occasionally.
After 30 mins test to ensure onions are soft. If not, cook another 10 mins.
Remove garlic.

Turn the sweat into soup:
Add	stock
	S & P to taste.

Cook another 30 mins, covered.
Ladle into soup bowls, sprinkle
with parsley and top with optional   crouton
cheese.

Hearty Pea and Sausage Soup   SKILLET/SLOW COOKER

It is amazing how delicious and inexpensive a hearty soup can be. Try this recipe on a weekend since it takes a while to cook.

Gather together:
2 Cooked Sausages, spicy & smoked, e.g., kielbasa, cut in 1/2"/**1.25cm** pieces
Optional: 1 T/**15ml** Oil for sautéing
1 Potato, cut into small cubes
1 cooking Onion, chopped, to make 1/4 C/**60ml**
1 t/**5ml** fresh or 1/2 t/**2.5ml** Dried Rosemary, chopped
1/2 C/**120ml** Dried Split Peas, green or yellow, rinsed
1 1/2 C/**360ml** Chicken Broth from a can, box, or cube
Optional: **1** Carrot and **1** Celery rib, diced or sliced
Garnish: chopped Parsley

To make the soup on the stovetop:
Sauté (with oil if needed) in a heavy pot until fat begins to flow.	sausage pieces
Add	potato cubes onion rosemary optional carrot optional celery.
Sauté about 5 minutes on medium heat, stirring, to soften and develop flavour. Mix in	dried peas chicken broth.

Bring the soup to a boil, then simmer on low heat 60-90 minutes:
stirring occasionally, until peas are soft and breaking down.

Adjust thickness of soup.
If needed, add water.
Add to taste S & P.
Serve the soup in <u>heated</u> soup plates.
See microwave **TIP!** below.
<u>Garnish:</u>
each bowl with chopped parsley.

<u>This recipe may be done in your slow cooker:</u>
Be sure to put the onions, potatoes, carrots and celery on the **bottom** of the pot. Omit the oil. Cook for 4-5 hours on HIGH, stirring occasionally after the first hour if you can.

TIP! To make more soup, simply multiply the amounts of broth, peas and onion by 2 or 3. Add additional sausage as you choose and maybe one more potato. Be careful to add no more than 1 1/2 t/8ml fresh rosemary or 1 t/5ml dried rosemary because its flavour can become overwhelming. **When making the soup in a slow cooker, do not adjust the quantities of rosemary at all because its flavour intensifies too much.**

TIP! <u>Add mushrooms</u> if you like them. Chop them roughly, then sauté them in a bit of butter over med-high heat until they are brown and have released their moisture. Put the cooked mushrooms into the soup just before serving time.

TIP! Heating soup bowls in the micro takes about one minute for a stack of two to four. Heat on HIGH for 1 min.
For a single soup bowl, put a little water in the bowl and heat for 30 secs to 1 min. Remember <u>not</u> to heat your grandmother's gold-rimmed soup plates in the micro!!!

Soups & Stews Dumplings

If you are serving a soup with vegetables and stock or a lovely soupy stew, why not dress it up with dumplings? These are made with instant polenta, a corn meal, so they add good nutrition for a complete meal.

Gather together:
1 1/4 C/**300ml** Water
1/2 C/**120ml** Instant Polenta (usually yellow or white cornmeal)
Garnish: shredded or grated Parmesan Cheese

Cook and Stir, then Cool:
In a pot bring to boiling	the water.
Add, lowering heat to simmer	the polenta.
Cook, stirring, 2 mins to thicken.	
Remove from the pot to a greased pan so the polenta can cool, and then shape polenta into round dumplings, using wet hands.	
Add dumplings to your soup or stew at its final heating.	
Heat the dish on med until steam rises to warm the dumplings.	
Serve in a wide bowl with if desired.	a Parmesan garnish

TIP! Do not use the ready-made polenta in a round roll. It really doesn't taste very good.

TIP! Supermarkets sell ready-made soups that can be made into a complete meal by adding polenta dumplings along with diced veggies from your fridge.

El.Wok/Frypan Recipes:
Beef Stroganoff for 1	66
Roasted Chicken for 1	75
Pan Fried Fish	80
Sausage Supper for 1	102
Simple Spicy Spareribs	103

Better Baked Beans	64
Beginner's Beefsteak Casserole for Company	65
Instant Beef Stroganoff for 1	66
'Asian' Chili Chicken for 2	67
Buttery Garlic Chicken Breasts for 2	68
Noodley Curried Chicken for 1	69
Creative Uses for BBQ Chicken	70
'Italian' Chicken Breasts for 2	72
Murielle's Parmesan Chicken for 4	74
Roasted Chicken for 1	75
Chinese-style Roast Chicken for 4	76
Southern Fried Chicken for 4	77
'French' Chicken Stew for 2	78
Pan Fried Fish Fillets	80
Foiled Fish	82
Fish & Seafood Cioppino for 2	83
Fish Pot Pie for 2	84
Frittata with Toast	86
Liver 'n Onions for 2	88
Saucy Meatballs for Company	90
Spicy Glazed Pork Chops for 2	91
Roasted Pork	92
Roasted Garlic Pork	93
Bacon & Bean Quesadillas	94
Chili Beef Quesadillas	95
Salmon in the Micro	96
Beth's Best Salmon Filet	97
John's Fried Scallops with Dill Sauce	98
Instant Garlic Shrimp	100
Salty and Sweet Shrimp for 2	101
Sausage Supper for 1	102
Simple Spicy Spareribs	103
Old Fashioned Tuna Casserole	104

Better Baked Beans

OVEN & SKILLET/SLOW COOKER & SKILLET

Canned baked beans are quite tasty but your own additions do improve their taste. The bacon adds a nice smoky flavour but it is not absolutely necessary. This recipe serves 2 at least.

<u>Gather together:</u>
15oz/**425g** can Baked Beans
2 T/**30ml** Brown Sugar
1/2 t/**2.5ml** Dry Mustard
1/4 C/**60ml** Ketchup
if desired, **4-5** strips Bacon, cut in half

<u>Put it together:</u>
Into a skillet mix together   all ingredients
                                        <u>except</u> bacon.

Arrange over top   bacon strips.
<u>Bake</u> at 350/180:
about 30 mins until
bacon is cooked to your liking.

<u>For the slow cooker:</u>
Place into the pot   all ingredients
                                        <u>except</u> bacon.

Heat on HIGH for 1 1/2 - 2 hours.
Then stir well but gently to avoid
breaking the soft beans.
Using a skillet or microwave cook   bacon.
Serve beans and top beans with   cooked bacon.

Make-a-meal: Toast whole wheat English muffins and add a salad of greens and crisp veggies with tomatoes.

Beginner's Steak Casserole for Company

This recipe makes a one dish meal that is tasty, hearty and a no-brainer. Just don't freeze it and then forget to let it thaw before heating (unless you like frozen spaghetti!).

Gather together:
1/3 pkg/about **150g** Spaghetti or Spaghettini
1 T/**15ml** Butter + **dash** Oil
1/2 lb/**225g** Ground Roundsteak or Sirloin Steak
1/2 Spanish Onion, chopped
1/2 large Green Pepper, chopped
1/2 lb/**225g** Mushrooms, quartered
1/2 10oz can condensed Tomato Soup
1/2 19oz can/**270ml** Diced Tomatoes
1/3 lb/**150g** grated Cheese, preferably cheddar

Cook the spaghetti:
Cook in salted water to 'al dente' about 7 mins. Drain.	the spaghetti

Put steak, veg and cheese together:
In a large oven skillet with lid, heat	butter and oil.
Sauté to soften	green pepper mushrooms onions.
Remove the veggies. In the same pan brown lightly Return veggies to the pan.	ground steak.
Stir in	tomato soup tomatoes.
Fold in	cheese & spaghetti.

Cover and bake at 350/180:
about 30 mins until hot and bubbling
  − in the middle too.

Instant Beef Stroganoff for 1+   STOVE/ EL.WOK/FRYPAN

Stroganoff used to be a party dish because it includes 'exotic' sour cream and tender beef. Imagine! For additional servings, multiply ingredients. Just make sure you do not crowd the beef when cooking...you may need to brown the meat in batches.

Gather together:
1 T/**15ml** Butter + 1 T/**15ml** Oil
1/2 medium Onion, sliced or diced
Tender Beef, cut into strips about 1/2" by 2"/**1.25x5 cm**, the right amount for you, dried with paper towels
2 stems fresh Parsley + more for garnish
2 Gherkins (sour pickles), chopped fine + more for garnish
about 2 T/**30ml** Sour Cream
1/2 Lemon, grated for zest and then squeezed for juice
Hot Cooked Rice, the right amount for you (use about 1/3 C/**80ml** raw rice) or Cooked Egg Noodles, **1** handful

Fry and stir:
In a frypan/wok on med, heat   butter and oil.
Add and cook to light brown   onion slices.
Turn up heat to <u>med-high</u> and add beef cooking quickly, stirring, to just brown beef on all sides.
Stir in the   parsley
                                            chopped gherkins
                                            lemon zest & juice.
Stir in quickly   sour cream.
Completely heat the Stroganoff:
Just heat, do not boil.
Ladle Stroganoff over hot rice or noodles and garnish with more parsley and gherkins.

'Asian' Chili Chicken for 2

This recipe is a take-off on the usual recipe for General Tso's Chicken. It is easy, quick and tasty. You'll want to serve it over noodles or rice to mop up the sticky juices.

Gather together:
4 pieces Chicken Leg seasoned with Salt
2 T/**30ml** Oil
1 T/**15ml** Asian Chili-Garlic Sauce
1/4 C/**60ml** Chicken Broth
1/2 C/**120ml** White Sugar
1 T/**15ml** Water

Bake the chicken at 350F/180C:
Place on a baking pan   the chicken legs
and drizzle them with   oil.
Bake chicken until brown and
cooked, about 30 mins.
Drain the chicken on paper towels.
Combine in a bowl: chili-garlic sauce
                                                chicken broth.

Make the sticky sauce:
In a small but deep pan stir together   sugar and water.
Without stirring, heat on medium   sugar mixture
until it turns to caramel, swirling
the pan to prevent burning.
Remove the pan from the heat.
Put it all together:
Stir into the caramel   chili-garlic broth
(keep away from the steam!)
and add   the chicken
stirring, to coat it with   caramel sauce.

Buttery Garlic Chicken Breasts for 2
A buttermilk bath makes chicken tender and juicy. See p.45 for condiments to further jazz up the chicken.

Gather together:
2 Boneless, Skinless Chicken Breasts
1 C +/**240ml +** Buttermilk, enough to cover the chicken
1/2 to 3/4 C/**120-180ml** Fine Bread Crumbs, depending on size of the breasts
1/4 C/**60ml** Parmesan Cheese, grated
2 small Garlic cloves, finely minced
freshly ground P & S
2 T/**30ml** Butter

Put Chicken in its bath:
Immerse the breasts in buttermilk.
Place in the fridge for at least one hour.
Prepare the breasts:
Shake off the buttermilk (dispose of it).
Mix the coating together and dip chicken:
Combine fine crumbs
Parmesan, garlic
2 grinds P, **pinch** S.
Dip in crumbs each chicken piece.
Reserve remaining crumbs.
Sauté chicken:
Heat on med in an oven safe pan butter.
When butter sizzles add chicken.
Brown on one side, then turn over.
Coat the already browned side with remaining crumbs.
Bake in a 425F/220C oven:
for 10-15 mins until chicken is tender.

Noodley Curried Chicken **for 1**
Simple, straightforward and quick. What's not to like?

Gather together:
1/2 C/**120ml** <u>cooked</u> Egg Noodles (freeze any left-overs)
1/4 C/**60ml** noodle water
1/2 T/**8ml** Oil
1/2 Chicken Breast, cut into thin strips
2 slices Onion
pinch or two hot Red Pepper flakes
1/2 to1 t/**2.5 to 5ml** sliced and minced Gingerroot
1-2 t/**5-10ml** Curry Powder
Garnish: chopped Peanuts
       thinly sliced fresh Spinach

Sauté away:
In a small skillet heat on med	oil.
Add and stir and cook 3 mins	chicken strips.
Remove chicken to a warm plate.	
Add and soften on low heat 8 mins	onion slices.
Add and stir and cook 2 mins	hot pepper flakes
	ginger
	curry powder.
Stir in	noodles
	noodle water
	chicken

and reheat briefly.
Dump into a bowl, garnish and enjoy.

TIP! This recipe makes a tasty soup too. Simply add 1/2-1 C/**120-240ml or more** of chicken broth. Check seasoning and perhaps add more ginger or a garlic clove.

Simple Uses for BBQ Chicken

Below are a few ideas for left-over BBQ roasted chicken. It's a good buy and it usually tastes pretty good.

Chicken Salad	Combine cubes of chicken with mayo, celery, green onion, grapes, sliced almonds.
Chicken with Pasta	Cook the pasta and drain it. Heat your favourite pasta sauce and then add and stir in the pasta plus shreds or cubes of chicken.
Chicken Tacos	Using a taco kit, substitute shredded chicken for the meat called for in the package.
Chicken Quesadilla	Grill a flour tortilla for a min or two. Cover ungrilled side with chicken shreds, cheese, green pepper slices, sliced olives. Fold the tortilla over once, then again. Return the filled tortilla to the grill pan and heat briefly to melt the cheese.
Chicken Sandwich Wrap	Spread one half of a flat bread such as a flour tortilla with mayo. Cover that with sliced chicken. Dot with red pepper jelly, S & P. Cover with a lettuce leaf. Wrap it up.

Pizza with Chicken	Use your favourite flat bread. Spread a thin layer of mango chutney all over. Sprinkle that with olive oil. Cover with strips of chicken and cheese (provolone or cheddar or your choice). Dot with more chutney. Bake at 400F/200C for about 15 mins.
Chicken Noodle Soup	For an Asian version, use a packet of ramen + cubes or shreds of chicken + sliced green onions + dash of soy sauce.
Chicken & Rice Soup	Start with a small can of ready-to-use mushroom soup. Stir in about 1 1/2 T/**22ml** uncooked rice. Cover and simmer 20 mins. Add chicken bits. Spice it up with 1/4 t/**1.25ml** lemon pepper. Do not add salt.
Chicken Curry	A jar of good curry sauce from the supermarket will infuse pieces of chicken (skin off) with a lovely flavour. Adding some fruit such as mango, banana, apple, grapes or raisins improves the dish by adding a sweet smoothness. Serve the sauce over hot rice.

'Italian' Chicken Breasts for 2

The lusty flavours of this easy-to-prepare dish are perfect for that once-in-a-while special little dinner.

Gather together:
2 small Chicken Breasts
2 large or 4 small thin slices Prosciutto
2 heaping T/**30ml+** shredded Cheese – Cheddar, Asiago, Provolone
Optional: store-bought Pesto, about 2 T/**30ml**
S & P if desired

Prepare the breasts:
Place on a washable cutting board the breasts.
Using a sharp thin blade,
slice horizontally into the thicker side of each breast, being careful not to cut all the way through.
Open each breast like a book.

Fill and bake at 375F/190C:
Spread onto each open breast pesto if using shredded cheese.

Close the 'books'.
Spread out on a baking pan prosciutto slices and place on top a filled breast.
Tightly roll up each breast in the prosciutto, keeping all the filling enclosed, using toothpicks if necessary.

Bake:
for 30 mins, until juices run clear.

73

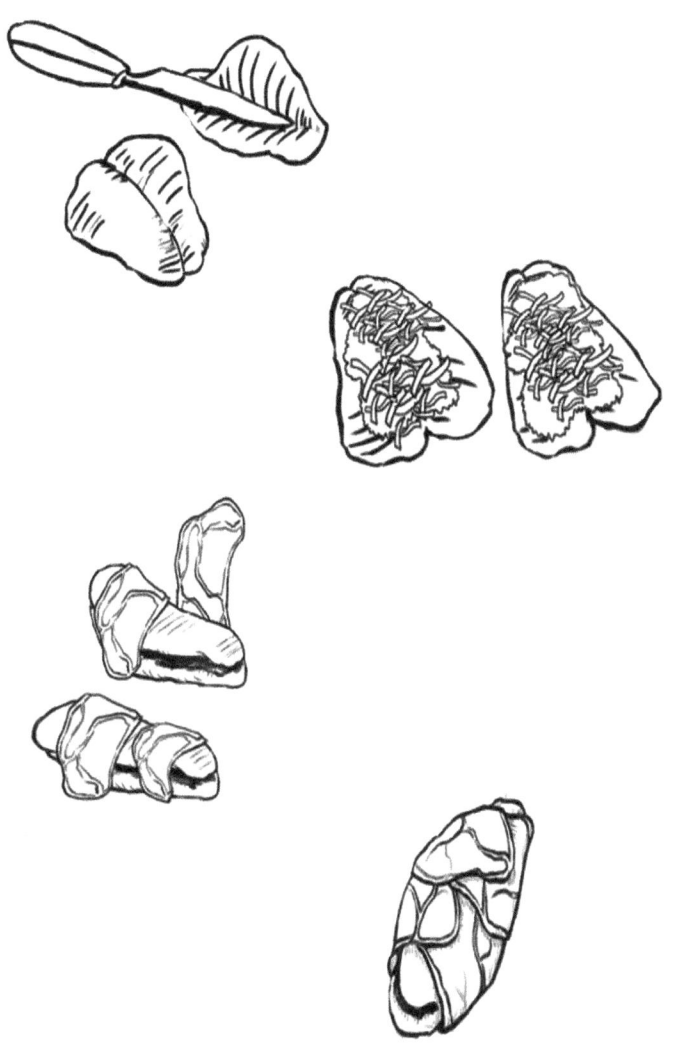

Murielle's Parmesan Chicken for 4
So simple! So tasty! So fast!

Gather together:
1 can (680 ml) or jar zesty Pasta Sauce
4 T/**60ml** grated Parmesan Cheese **divided in 2 parts**
4 small Chicken Breasts, boneless, skinless **or 2 large** breasts cut in half lengthwise
1 C/**240ml** shredded Mozzarella Cheese
Tinfoil

Prepare in 2 mins:
Turn the oven or toaster oven to 375F/190C.
Stir together sauce
2 T/**30ml** Parmesan.

Add and turn to coat with sauce the chicken.
Place chicken in baking dish that just fits the amount of chicken.
Cook covered and uncovered:
Cover the dish closely with foil.
Bake for 30 mins.
Uncover the dish.
Top the chicken with mozzarella & remaining 2T /**30ml** Parmesan.

Bake another 5-10 mins to finish cooking the chicken (until juices run clear) and melt the cheeses. Serve over hot cooked pasta.

Roasted Chicken for 1   OVEN/TOASTER OVEN/ EL.WOK/FRYPAN

Even when cooking just for yourself it is possible to enjoy roasted meats. Here is a way to prepare roast chicken that makes the chicken juicy and savoury.

Gather together:
1 Chicken Thigh & Drumstick or 1 Breast with bones and skin
1/2 Lemon, roughly chopped
1 small Green Onion, chopped
1 clove Garlic, minced
S & freshly ground P
1 strip Bacon
Juice of **1/2** Lemon
A foil-lined baking tray, greased, OR grease the wok
Optional: **dashes** of Balsamic Vinegar and Orange Juice
+ 2 T/**30ml or so** of Water

'Stuff' the chicken:
Make a mixture of the   lemon, onion, garlic,
                                         S & P.

Mound it in the centre of the foil/wok.
Drape overtop   chicken pieces
and over that drape   bacon.
Cover chicken loosely with foil.
Roast at 375F/190C:
for 30 mins or until juices run clear.
For wok cooking, use med heat, 15 mins.
Remove   bacon & foil.
Squeeze all over chicken   lemon juice.
Return chicken to the oven/wok 3-5 mins.
Optionally, add and stir in   balsamic, orange
                                         juice and water

to create a sauce.

Chinese-style Roast Chicken for 4
Here is a roasting method that produces a juicy and flavour-filled bird. To serve, chop chicken into pieces instead of slicing.

Gather together:
1 small (**1.5-2 k**) Chicken
1 stalk Lemon Grass (using tender end) OR **1** Lemon or Lime
1/2 inch/**1.27cm** Gingerroot, peeled and minced
2 cloves Garlic, minced
3 T/**45ml** roughly chopped Cilantro leaves
1 T/**15ml** Soy sauce
1 T/**15ml** Oil
about 1 t/**5ml** Asian chili-garlic paste/ sauce, to your taste
about 1/2 C/**120ml** White Wine
1 T/**15ml** Butter

Mix up the Flavour Paste:
Chop fine and mix together	tender part of a stalk of lemon grass Or, juice of lemon or lime & 1 T/**15ml** zest ginger, garlic cilantro leaves.
Add and the	oil, soy sauce chili paste/sauce.

Spread flavour paste over entire chicken and under the skin where possible.
Place chicken on a rack on a baking pan and Roast at 400F/200C for 30 mins:
Reduce heat to 325F/190C and Roast another 30-45 mins:
Check for doneness (when juices run clear).
For 'jus', stir into juices and boil	wine.
Add and stir in to combine	butter.

Southern Fried Chicken for 4

Making fried chicken at home is something of a lost art. It is not difficult, it's inexpensive, and you'll be glad you tried it.

Gather together:
Skinless Chicken pieces including breasts cut across, thighs and legs, **enough to feed 4**
Buttermilk, well shaken, **enough to cover** chicken
1 C/**240ml** Flour + S & P
Paper bag for shaking chicken in flour
Canola Oil & Shortening, half and half, measuring
1 1/2"/**3.75cm deep** in the skillet

Here's how:
In a shallow bowl, marinate the   chicken pieces in buttermilk.
Let rest at least 1 hour in fridge.
Drain and pat chicken dry.
Bread the chicken:
Shake in the paper bag   flour + S & P.
Add to the bag   pieces of chicken
and shake the bag well.
Knock excess flour off chicken.
Heat the oil and shortening to 360/182 degrees:
(when oil bubbles up around the
handle of a wooden spoon !)
Fry the breaded chicken:
Carefully slide into hot oil   each chicken piece
and immediately cover the pan.
Let chicken fry about 5 mins to gold.
Turn over and fry another 3-5 mins.
Stab a piece to see that juices run 'clear'.
Drain on paper towels and keep warm.

'French' Chicken Stew for 2   SKILLET + SLOW COOKER

This recipe is for a Slow Cooker so you can be sure it is simple but delicious. The finished dish may be frozen.

Gather together:
4-6 Chicken Thighs
2 T/**30ml** Oil
1 Onion, sliced
1 T/**15ml** good Mustard such as Dijon
1/2 t/**2.5ml** dried Thyme
1 T/**15ml** crumbled Sage leaves
S & P
1/4 C/**60ml** Sherry
1 T/**15ml** Flour, preferably <u>Instant</u>
Cold Water

First, brown the chicken:
Heat a skillet on med-high
and add the   oil.
Sprinkle the thighs with   S & P.
and brown them all over in the oil.
Second, spice up the onions:
Mix together the   mustard and spices
and mix in with the   onions.
Layer in the slow cooker: half the onions,
    half the chicken,
    the rest of the
    onions,
    remaining thighs.
Pour over top   the sherry.
Cover the cooker and set to LOW
for 4-5 hours or HIGH for about 3 hours.

Try to turn over the ingredients at least once during the cooking.
To thicken the stew, mix instant flour with a bit of cold water.
Stir into stew and let cook, <u>uncovered</u>, about 30 mins.

Pan Fried Fish Fillets STOVE/EL.WOK/FRYPAN

Do not be leery of frying fish. It's really simple! That's a promise. And this method of cooking makes lovely moist fish.

Gather together:
1, 2, 3 or 4 Fillets of White Fish, about 1/2"/**1.3cm thick**, either completely skinned or with skin remaining on one side. For filets with skin, make 2 slashes through the skin so the flesh cooks evenly. Dry each fillet with paper towels.
2-3 T/**30-45ml** Flour for dredging the fish
1 t/**5ml** fine Herbs – fresh chives/ lemon thyme/parsley/dill
1-2 T/**15-30ml** Vegetable Oil
1-2 T/**15-30ml** Butter
sprinkle of Salt and White Pepper
1 T/**15ml** minced Chives for garnish
Lemon wedges for garnish

Prepare the fish:

On a large piece of plastic/paper mix	flour
	herbs.
Dip each piece of fish in	flour mixture
then shake to remove excess flour.	

Fry:

In a shallow pan on med-high OR in an el.wok on med, melt until melted and bubbling.	oil and butter
Slide into pan, not touching, (Fish may need to be cooked in two batches so that the fillets fry crisply, not braise or stew in their own juices.)	fillets.
Sprinkle each fillet with	S & P.
Fry without moving fish for 2 to 3 minutes, until first side is brown.	

Carefully lift each fillet with a long
spatula and turn fillet over.
Sprinkle that side with S & P.
Cook until the fillet flakes easily
when gently prodded with a fork,
1-2 mins. Do not overcook!
Remove fillets to a heated plate and
keep warm while remaining fillets cook.
Garnish fish with lemon wedges.

Make-a-Meal: Serve with Mediterranean roasted potatoes (p.33), mashed potatoes or herbed rice plus one or two coloured vegetables and/or salad.

TIP! When cooking fillets of fish that have skin remaining on one side, put the skin side down first on the pan. Your objective is to create a crispy skin. And don't forget to make slashes in the skin for even cooking of the flesh.

TIP! Cold-water fish such as salmon provide the greatest bioactive source of OMEGA-3 fatty acids. They are important for a healthy heart at all ages and they may help to reduce anxiety and depression in young adults. For older people, these acids help prevent macular degeneration.

Special Equipment: A spatula made especially for fish, long and curved slightly with a wide end, helps to keep the fish in one piece when it is moved or transferred.

Foiled Fish – a method recipe
Here is a useful method for any firm fish and any number of servings. The recipe below serves one.

Gather together:
Rectangles of Tinfoil, large enough to make a package around each piece of fish
1 piece of Firm Fish per serving – salmon, flounder, halibut
1 t/**5ml** Soft Butter for foil + 1 t/**5ml** Butter to top the fish
1/2 t/**2.5ml** Herbs to your taste – sage, rosemary & thyme
sprinkle of S & P
sprinkle of Garlic Powder

Make a fish package:
Spread on the centre of the tinfoil	butter.
Place in the middle of the foil	piece of fish.
Adorn the fish with sprinkles of	herbs
	S & P
	garlic powder.
Top the fish with a	pat of butter.

Fold the tinfoil into a well sealed but loose package.
Bake the package(s) at 400F/200C **for 13 mins exactly**.

Make-a-Meal: Why not use your hot oven to roast olive-oiled 'fries' and tomato halves to make a complete dinner along with a green salad? The fries would need to go into the oven 30 mins before the fish, and the tomatoes 10 mins before.

Fish & Seafood Cioppino for 2 — SLOW COOKER

This zesty, flavourful West coast recipe is great in a slow-cooker/crock pot. If cioppino is made on the stove the timing will be significantly less. For example, the vegetables and stock will need only about 30 mins on med-low and the fish and shrimp together need just 3 mins on a stove-top. For 4 servings, simply double the quantities.

Gather together:
1/4 Onion, sliced
2 t/**10ml** minced Garlic
2 t/**10ml** minced fresh Ginger
pinch Red Pepper Flakes
1/4 t/**1.25ml** dried Thyme leaves
1 1/2 C/**360ml** Clamato Juice OR 1 C/240ml Tomato juice + 1/2C/120ml Clam juice (supermarket)
1/4 t/1.25ml White Pepper
1 t/**5ml** grated Lime zest + 1 T/**15ml** lime juice
1/2 C/**120ml** bite-sized firm Fish
1/4 C/**60ml** ready-to-cook medium Shrimp

Place in a Crock Pot:
All ingredients <u>except</u>   lime, fish, shrimp.
Turn pot to HIGH heat setting and leave, covered, about 2 hours.
<u>10 mins before serving</u>:
Return heat to HIGH and when stock
Is bubbling gently add   lime zest and juice
                                                 fish.

Cook on HIGH, covered, 3 mins.
Add   shrimp.
Cook on High about 2 mins, just until shrimp turns pink.

Fish Pot Pie for 2
Quick to make, delicious to eat and almost a meal in one dish.

Gather together:
3 T/**45ml** Butter
1 medium Onion, chopped
2 T/**30ml** Flour
1/4 C/**60ml** White Wine or Vermouth
1/2 C/**120ml** Fish Broth (use a packet or a bullion cube)
1/4-1/3 C/**60-80ml** Heavy Cream
Total of 1 C/**240ml** sliced Veggies: Carrots (very thin), Celery, Mushrooms + Fennel stalks if desired
1 Lemon for Juice
1 C/**240ml** bite-sized pieces uncooked fish, scallops, shrimp – all about the same size
1 sheet frozen Puff Pastry, thawed but cold
1 Egg, beaten

Sauté away:
In a large frypan melt on medium heat	butter.
Add and sweat but do not brown	onions.
Stir in and cook for 2 mins	flour.
Stir in and cook for 1 min	wine.
Stir in	fish broth
	cream.
Simmer, stirring occasionally, 5 mins.	
Add	vegetables.
Cover the pan and cook on low about 10 mins until vegetables are tender.	

Prepare and cook fish, scallops, shrimp:
Squeeze over the fish	juice of the lemon
and then add to the pan	fish, scallops and shrimp.

Cover and cook about 5 mins until
shrimp are just pink. (overcooking = tough!)
<u>Make the pie:</u>
Ladle into 2 individual
casserole dishes or 1 large dish   the filling.
Cut to size+ with scissors   puff pastry
(the pastry should be large enough
to overhang the rim).
Press pastry outside the top of rim
with your fingers.
Brush the pastry with   beaten egg.
Make one or two slashes in the pastry top.
<u>Bake in a 400F/200C oven:</u>
for about 20 mins until pastry is golden
and filling bubbles. For most ovens,
use the middle rack to cook the pastry
properly.

Make-a-Meal: Add a crisp green salad with a zingy dressing.

TIP! This recipe teaches you the wonders of puff pastry. One wonder is that it is useful for many toppings. Another wonder is that it only behaves when it is COLD, before and after working with it. Covering the pastry with a light bag of frozen stuff while you work will do the trick. Or dampen a clean towel, fold it to the same size as the pastry sheet, cool it in the fridge and use it to cover the pastry when it is out of the fridge. By the way, thawing frozen puff pastry takes a couple of hours out of the fridge.

Frittata with Toast

A frittata is easier to make than an omelet, so it is a good choice for a company lunch or a quick supper. The toast adds texture underneath the eggs. This recipe serves 4.

Gather together
1 T/**15ml** Oil + 1 T/**15ml** Butter
1 medium Onion, sliced thin
1 T/**15ml** fresh Herbs, minced – thyme/lemon thyme/chives/parsley/marjoram or a mixture
1 large Tomato, chopped, then drained of excess juice
S & P
6 large Eggs **or 8 medium** Eggs, beaten lightly
1/2 C/**120ml** shredded sharp Cheese such as old cheddar
4 slices hearty Bread, crusts removed
Butter for the toast

Melt, cook, broil:

In an oven-ready skillet melt on med	oil and butter.
When foam subsides, stir in	onions
and cook, stirring occasionally until onions are soft and a bit browned.	
Stir in	herbs
	tomato.
Sprinkle with	S & P.
Cook veggies together for about 5 mins to soften and thicken.	
Pour in (and swirl pan)	eggs.
Cook on med, just to set, about 6 mins. **Do not stir.**	
Sprinkle over top	cheese
and broil on high 2 mins, to melt the cheese. Watch it!	

Toast:
Meanwhile, toast	4 slices bread.
Lightly spread the toast with	butter.
Place a toast on each plate (warmed) and top with	a slice of frittata.

TIP! To easily remove seeds and juice from a tomato, cut it into halves or quarters. Over the sink or a 'garbage pot' or compost pail, gently squeeze each piece. Voila! The seeds and juice are gone.

Liver 'n Onions for 2

Don't be afraid to attempt this quick meal. Use veal liver for a smooth taste. The classic partner for liver is mashed potatoes, preferably with garlic, and the classic garnish is a golden tangle of caramelized onions.

Gather together:
2 thin slices Veal Liver, about 6"/**15cm** long
Milk, as a bath for the liver
Oil & Butter, about 1 T/**15ml** in all for sautéing onions
1 Onion, thinly sliced
Oil & Butter, about 2 T/**30ml** in all for cooking liver
Flour, enough to cover the bottom of a pie plate
S & P
Red wine or Vermouth, about 1/3 C/**80ml** for sauce
1-2 t/**5-10ml** Butter for sauce

Marinate the liver:

In a shallow bowl cover liver with	milk
Let marinate in the fridge while onions cook.	

Cook onions:

In a skillet heated on medium put	first amount oil & butter.
Add and stir in	onion slices.
Reduce heat to low. Stir occasionally while onions caramelize, about 15 mins. Remove onions and keep them warm.	

Prepare liver and sauté:

Add to the skillet on med-high heat	second amount oil and butter.
Dip into the plate of flour	one piece of liver at a time.

Shake off excess flour.
Slide into the hot skillet   the liver.
Sprinkle liver with   S & P.
Quickly cook on first side, about
1 min only, then turn liver over.
Sprinkle second side of liver with   S & P
and brown quickly.
* The liver is now cooked! Please do not overcook liver, as it turns mealy and becomes dry.*
Remove liver from skillet
to a warm plate.

<u>Make the sauce:</u>
Deglaze the skillet with   red wine or vermouth.
Let wine boil briefly.
Finish sauce by swirling in   1-2 t/**5-10ml** butter.
Serve liver topped with pan gravy,
then a tangle of onions.

Make-a-Meal: For the classic liver 'n onions meal, prepare mashed potatoes before cooking the liver. When ready to serve, reheat the potatoes in the micro, 1-2 mins on HIGH.

Add Spinach! Creamed spinach is a superior accompaniment. It can be prepared quickly by defrosting and squeezing dry a **box** of frozen chopped spinach and adding it to a pan of 1/2 C/**120ml** cream, simmering with 1/4 C/**60ml** chopped shallots or red onion. Let the spinach simmer in the cream about 3 mins, stirring.

Saucy Meatballs for Company　　　SKILLET/SLOW COOKER

This recipe is for a slow cooker on a lazy weekend since it takes time but makes a scrumptious meal. Or use a skillet for relative speed. The recipe will also create a special hot meatball dish to go with drinks – make the balls tiny and provide toothpicks or cocktail forks.

Gather together:
1 lb/**455g** Italian Meatballs OR 1 lb/**455g** ground Turkey
1 t/**5ml** Garlic Powder with herbs (or mix up your own)
S & P
Store bought Sweet and Sour Sauce OR mix your own, **below:**
1 large can Tomato Sauce, **about** 2 C/480 ml
1/2 C/**120ml** Chili Sauce
1/4 C/**60ml** Vinegar
1/4 C/**60ml** Brown Sugar

In a slow cooker OR
in a deep heavy skillet with a lid:
place　　　　　　　　　　　　　　store sauce
OR mix together　　　　　　　　　sauce ingredients
and put into the skillet.
Prepare the meatballs:
Mix together gently　　　　　　　turkey, garlic, S & P
and form the meat into small balls.
OR
Sprinkle ready-made meatballs with　　garlic powder, S & P.
Gently put meat balls in the sauce and:
cover the slow cooker or skillet.
In a slow cooker heat on LOW for 4-5 hours or 2-3 hours on HIGH
Or for a skillet
simmer on the stove for an hour, stirring occasionally.

Spicy Glazed Pork Chops for 2

This very quick-cooking pork recipe has an Asian twist. It is wonderful with rice, perhaps the Orange Rice, page 36?

Gather together:
2 Pork Chops, preferably bone-in, 1/2"/**1.27cm thick**
S & P
1 T/**15ml** Oil
For the Sauce:
2 T/**30ml** Soy sauce
1 T/**15ml** Sugar
1 T/**15ml** Orange Juice
1 t/**5ml** Orange Zest
1 t (heaping)/**5ml+** Gingerroot, minced
1 t (heaping)/**5ml+** Garlic, minced
1/2 t/**2.5ml** Cornstarch
dash Red Pepper flakes (or more)
1/4C/**60ml** Water

Cook the chops:
Dry the chops and sprinkle with   S & P.
Heat a large skillet on med-high
and add   oil.
Brown 3 mins each side   the chops
(longer for thicker chops).   .
Transfer chops to a warm plate.
Glaze:
Whisk together for the sauce   all remaining ingredients.

Pour off fat from the skillet.
Deglaze the pan with   the water.
Stir in and simmer to thicken   the sauce.
Return chops to skillet to reheat/glaze.

Roasted Pork

Pork is often an economy cut of meat, easy to find, easy to cook and delicious to eat as long as it is not overcooked. Left overs make a sandwich or can be stir fried for another meal.

Gather together:
2-3 lb (**1-1.5kg**) Pork Roast, loin or rib
1 sprig fresh Rosemary, leaves removed and chopped
1 t/**5ml** dried Thyme, crushed
S & P
1 T/**15ml** Olive Oil
splash White Wine
1/4 C/**60ml** Beef or Chicken Stock

Prepare the meat:
If the roast has a layer of fat, score
it with a sharp knife.
Rub roast all over with   rosemary, thyme,
                                           S & P.

Sear the roast:
Heat a roasting pan on med-high.
Add and let come to a sizzle   olive oil.
Sear all sides of the   pork roast
to a golden brown, about 10 mins.

Roast the roast at 350F/180C:
Place on a rack in the roasting pan   pork roast.
Cook for 45 mins, then test
for doneness by cutting a small slit
into centre of the meat. It should be
slightly pink, but not at all red.
After cooking let pork rest at least 10 mins,
on a platter tented with foil, then slice.

Make sauce:
On the stovetop, heat roasting pan.
Add and stir to deglaze pan   wine and stock.
Make sure all the brown bits are stirred
up and let sauce boil down to about
one-half volume.
Slice pork and ladle sauce over top.

Roasted Garlic Pork
This is more flavourful and sophisticated than the rather plain recipe above.

Gather together:
at least 2 Garlic Cloves, peeled and sliced thin
Grainy Mustard, about 2 T/**30ml**
Fine Bread Crumbs, fresh or dry, about 1/2 C/**120ml**
pinch or 2 of Thyme and Ground Sage

When preparing the meat:
Sprinkle meat with   S & P.
Make slashes on all sides of roast
and press in slivers of   garlic.
Slather top of roast with   mustard.
Coat with a mix of   crumbs,
                                      thyme, sage.
Drizzle with oil.
Roast as for previous recipe.

TIP! Fresh herbs are lovely to have in your kitchen but they don't keep well. To store them, wrap the washed herbs in a double layer of paper towels and then in a plastic bag in your crisper. Or place washed herbs, stems down, in a glass with a bit of water and try not to knock the glass over in the fridge.

Bacon & Bean Quesadillas

These are fun to make as well as yummy to eat. You may vary the ingredients but always use onions and cheese.

Gather together:
Squirt of Oil
2 large or 4 small soft Wheat Tortillas, your choice
small tub of Soft Cream Cheese, plain or with peppers
1/3 C/**80ml** canned Black Beans, rinsed in hot water
3 slices Bacon, fried and crumbled (use the micro, 2-3 mins)
1/2 C/**120ml** Onions, sliced and fried to soften or
fried longer to a golden colour
Hot Sauce, as you wish
small handful Monterey Jack/cheddar Cheese, shredded
Garnishes   Sour Cream and Tomato Salsa

Layer and quickly cook:
Heat on your grill/fry pan   oil.
Layer all ingredients on   one tortilla
in the order set out above.
Top with   a second tortilla.
Grill on med-high   the quesadilla.
until cheese melts and tortillas are crisp.
(Peek at the bottom and when it crisps
up, flip tortilla over).
Cut and serve:
Cut the large quesadilla into halves
and then cut each half into thirds,
using 3 pieces for each plate OR
place one small quesadilla cut into
thirds on each plate.
Serve with garnish, small bowls of   sour cream
                                      and salsa.

Chili Beef Quesadillas

Here is an oven baked recipe for a protein-rich, spicy filling in flour tortillas. Left over filling can be recycled with extra beans and tomatoes to make chili con carne.

Gather together:
1 T/**15ml** Oil
about 1/2 lb/**225g** pkg Ground Beef (lean) or Chicken
1 T/**15ml** Chili Powder
1/2 C/**120ml** Refried Beans from a can
1/2 C/**120ml** shredded pizza Cheese of your choice
1/2 C/**120ml** Salsa, mild or hot, your choice
1-2 Green Onions, chopped
1 pkg Flour Tortillas, large or small, preferably fried briefly

Make the filling:
Into a large frypan pour	oil.
Heat to shimmering and add	ground meat.
Turn heat to med and stir meat to break up lumps and brown.	
Sprinkle over meat	chili powder.
When meat is browned all over remove pan from heat.	
Drain off excess	oil.
Add and stir in	refried beans cheese, salsa green onions.

Fill tortillas and bake at 450C/230C:
On a cookie sheet place	4 tortillas.
Ladle on top of each 1/2 C+/- /**120ml** +/-	filling.
Top with	4 more tortillas.
To reheat filling, bake 10-15mins.	
Let rest 5 mins before cutting.	

Salmon in the Micro

Microwave ovens are true timesavers for certain classes of foods. These are foods whose elements can be broken down/cooked without changing their essential nature. Their nutrients are definitely retained and their colour is palatable to our 21st century tastes. Fish is definitely one of these foods.

Gather together:
Salmon steaks or filets, **enough for 1 or 2**
1/2 t/**2.5ml** S & freshly ground Pepper
Old Bay Seasoning, 1/2 to 1 t/**2.5-5ml**
dab of Butter **or dash** of Olive Oil
Lemons, to make 2-3 wedges per serving
Tartar Sauce, if desired as a condiment

Prepare the salmon:
Sprinkle salmon on both sides with	salt
	grind of pepper
	Old Bay.
In a single layer in a shallow dish put	salmon.
Top each piece with	butter/olive oil.

Cook on HIGH 2 1/2 mins:
depending on your machine's wattage.
Check for doneness by inserting fork
and looking for beginning of flakes.
Also, some white liquid from the fish
will start to appear.
Let the fish rest about 3 mins.

Serve with	lemon wedges
	tartar sauce.

TIP! Stir together chopped dill pickles, mayo. mustard and fresh lemon juice + hot sauce to make an easy tartar sauce.

Beth's Best Salmon Filet

The addition of a sauce or, in this case salsa, to a piece of salmon makes the dish special to look at as well as delicious to eat. It's 'Heart Smart' too. Freeze left over salsa if you prepare this recipe for just 1 or 2 servings.

Gather together:
1 Fillet of Salmon, (or 2) making sure bones are out, and slashing the skin if it remains on the fillet
1 Mango, diced
1 small Red Onion, diced small
1 fresh Tomato, diced
1/2 t/**2.5ml** each S & P
1 T/**15ml** Olive Oil

Make the Salsa:
Mix together	mango
	onion
	tomato.
Stir in	S & P
	olive oil.

Prepare the fish and salsa for the oven:
On a large piece of foil, spread	half the salsa.
Top this with	salmon filets.
Spread over the salmon pressing salsa down lightly.	remaining salsa,
Sprinkle overtop	olive oil.

Fold the foil into a tent-like package and place the tent on an oven tray.
Bake in a heated 400F/200C oven:
until the fish just begins to flake, 10-13 mins.

Serve with plenty of	salsa.

John's Fried Scallops with Dill Sauce
A wonderful dish, especially when scallops are on sale. 'Dry' scallops (shipped without preservatives) are best. For a company meal, simply multiply ingredient amounts.

Gather together:
4 large or 6 small Scallops (not Bay scallops) per serving
3 T/**45ml** Flour in a flattish dish
1-2 Eggs, beaten with a fork in a flattish bowl
1/2 C/**120ml** Plain Bread Crumbs on a plate large enough to hold all the scallops
1 t/**5ml** Fish Seasoning, e.g. Old Bay, stirred into the crumbs
Vegetable Oil, enough to cover a small frypan to half the height of the scallops
for Dill Sauce:
1/4 C/**60ml** Mayonnaise
1 T/**15ml** fresh Lemon Juice
1-2 T/**15-30ml** finely chopped Dill Pickles
dab of Mustard
S & P
3-5 drops Tabasco Sauce if a spicy sauce is desired

Make the sauce:
Combine the sauce ingredients and let the flavours meld in the fridge.
Prepare the scallops:
Line up on the counter the 3 dishes of flour,
eggs,
crumbs + seasoning.

One by one, dip scallops in flour, then egg then use your fingers to roll scallops in crumbs.

<u>Fry, drain, serve:</u>
Heat on med-high oil.
When it shimmers, gently add breaded scallops.
Fry until golden on bottom, 2 mins.
Turn and fry briefly to cook other side.
Remove and drain on paper towels.
Keep scallops warm in a 200F/100C oven.
Serve each plate with a big dollop of sauce on the side.

Make-a-Meal: Fried scallops with sauce go well with mashed potatoes or rice and sautéed spinach or green beans. A tomato/cucumber vinaigrette salad will complete a terrific meal.

Instant Garlic Shrimp

STOVE/ EL.WOK/FRYPAN

This recipe calls for cooked shrimp so the dish is truly instant and very garlicky. If you'd rather use uncooked shrimp, simply sauté them until they turn pink on both sides, 3 minutes only.

Gather together:
2 T/**30ml** Oil
1 T/**15ml** Butter
Jumbo peeled, deveined Cooked Shrimp, **about 5 per serving**
minced Garlic, 1 T/**15ml** per serving
minced Gingerroot, 1 t/**5ml** per serving
1/4 t /**1.25ml**+- Chili Pepper flakes per serving
splash of white Wine, about 1/4 C/**60ml** for 1 serving
chunk of Butter, about 1 T/**15ml**
S & P
Garnish: minced Parsley

Stir-fry:
In a frypan/wok heat on med-high	oil and butter.
Add and stir-fry 1-2 mins	shrimp.
Toss in and quickly stir	garlic, ginger, chili pepper.
Stir in and cook 30 secs	wine.
Stir in and cook 30 secs	butter.
Sprinkle with	S & P
	parsley, if using.

For a wok meal, cook the rice before the shrimp.

TIP! Rice is a good accompaniment since it soaks up the delicious garlic butter.

Salty and Sweet Shrimp for 2

These days, frozen shrimp are available in many sizes and degrees of readiness and they're not really expensive. They make a quick and tasty meal when they're not overcooked.

Gather together:
about 10 shrimp, depending on size, shelled and deveined (The largest size you can afford gives you the best value!)
1 T/**15ml** Oil
1-2 t/**5-10ml** finely chopped Garlic
1/2 small Onion, diced
1/4 t/**1.25ml** Asian Chili Sauce
3 Green Onions, sliced into 1"/**2.5cm** pieces
1/4 C/**60ml** Brown Sugar
2 T /**30ml** Fish Sauce (commonly available in supermarkets)
1/2 C/**120ml** Water

Make the caramel sauce:
Into a small pot place   sugar, fish sauce, water.

Boil until liquid is reduced by half.
Reserve this caramel sauce.
Cook the Shrimp:
In a frypan heat on med-high   oil.
Add and stir-fry to slight gold   onion
(this takes about 5 mins).
Add and stir-fry 30 secs   garlic.
Add   shrimp and sauce.
Stir-fry 2-3 mins to cook shrimp
until pink and curled while coating the
shrimp with the caramel sauce.
Stir in and toss around with shrimp   green onions.

Sausage Supper for 1
STOVE/ EL.WOK/FRYPAN

To feed 2 or more simply multiply the ingredients and find a skillet to fit. This dish is tasty and comes together in a flash.

Gather together:
1 or 2 fat Sausages, sweet or hot Italian for example, skin pierced several times with a fork
dash of Olive Oil
handful of Seedless Grapes
about 1/4 C/**60ml** sliced Onion
1/4 C/**60ml** Chicken or Beef Broth or Red Wine

Cook in a skillet/wok:
On medium heat cook	sausages
splashing them with	olive oil.
Let brown on all sides, 5 mins in a skillet, about 3 mins in an el.wok/frypan.	
Reduce heat to med-low and add	onions.
Let onions brown, stirring sometimes.	
Add to make a sauce	grapes and broth or wine.

Boil, allowing liquid to almost evaporate.
Serve sausages on top of the sauce.

Make-a-meal: Mashed potatoes or noodles plus broccoli and cauliflower florets that steam while the sausage cooks make a delicious and colourful meal. If using a wok, cook noodles before cooking sausages. Add noodles to the finished sausage dish to reheat briefly.

Simple Spicy Spareribs STOVE/ EL.WOK/FRYPAN

When the ribs are thin this recipe is a winner. With just four added ingredients, flavour is packed right into the meat and a glaze sparkles on the surface of the ribs.

Gather together:
4-6 rib Pork Spareribs
2-3 cloves Garlic, smashed and peeled
1/2 bottle Beer
1/2 C/**120ml** Water
2-3 T/**15-45ml** Red Pepper Jelly
1 t/**5ml** Garlic Powder

Steam the ribs:
Into a skillet with lid or wok place	water, beer, garlic cloves.
Add so meaty side is up	spareribs.

Bring liquid to a boil, turn down to simmer, cover and cook 45 mins. Turn ribs over. Off heat, let ribs cool in liquid, meaty side down. Drain liquid out.

Glaze and bake at 400F/200C:
Mix together	jelly and garlic powder.

Spoon it over meaty side of each rib. Bake on a foil-lined pan (for easy clean-up) for 30 mins or until glaze is hot and browned.
OR turn wok to med-low, cover wok and allow glaze to melt into ribs, about 5 mins.

Old Fashioned Tuna Casserole

This is an easy 1950's recipe that truly spells 'comfort'.

Gather together:
1/4 C/**60ml** Butter
1/4 C/**60ml** Flour
1 C/**240ml** Milk + 1 C/**240ml** light Cream
1/2 t/**2.5ml** S & 1/4 t/**1.25ml** freshly ground Pepper
1/2 C/**120ml** slivered Almonds, toasted in a dry pan
2T/**30ml** Butter for veggies
1 Onion, **1** Green Pepper, **1 rib** Celery, chopped
Broad Noodles, about 2 C/**480ml**, cooked in salted water
Tuna, **2 tins**, **totaling** about 12oz/**350g**, drained
big handful Buttered Bread Crumbs or Crushed Potato Chips

Make a white sauce:
Melt in saucepan on medium heat	butter.
Add, and stir 1-2 mins to cook	the flour.
Whisk in and bring just to a boil	milk, cream, S & P.
Remove from heat. Cool slightly.	

Cook the veggies:
On medium, in a dry pan, toast	slivered almonds.
Remove almonds and add to pan	butter for veggies.
Melt butter, add and cook to soften	chopped veggies.

Finish the Filling:
Combine with white sauce	almonds, veg, tuna.

Finish the Casserole:
Put in a buttered baking dish	noodles.
Top noodles with	tuna mixture
and sprinkle with	crumbs/chips.

Bake at 350F/180C:
about 30 min, until filling bubbles
and top is golden and crisp.

Sandwiches and Snacks

El.Wok/Frypan Recipes:	
Grilled Sandwiches	112
Your Own Hamburger	114
Your Own Hot Dog	117
Zippy Tortilla Nachos	120

Easy Canapés/hors d'oeuvres	106
Distinctive Dips	108
Garlic Bread with Herbs	109
Jazzed Up Pizzas	110
Grilled Sandwiches	112
Your Own Hamburger	114
Hammy Cheese Croissant	116
Your Own Hot Dog	117
Triscuit Toppers	118
Zippy Tortilla Nachos	120

Easy Canapés/hors d'oeuvres
Even the beginning cook can produce home-made goodies for a drinks party. Here are a few ultra-simple-to-make and tasty suggestions.

<u>Spicy Pita Crisps</u>
Brush melted butter or margarine over pita pockets that have been separated into two thin pieces.
Sprinkle with your choice(s): chili powder
garlic salt
lemon pepper
Parmesan cheese
sesame seeds
etc.
Place on baking sheet pita pieces
and cut into squares or triangles.
Bake at 225F/110C about 45 mins
until crisp.
Cool and store in an airtight container.

<u>Celery with ...</u>
Wash, dry, remove obvious strings on celery using a vegetable scraper, and cut celery into bite-sized lengths.
Mound into celery pieces: devilled ham from a can
devilled egg (cooked egg mixed
with mayo, mustard)
blue cheese, mashed
and topped with
chopped walnuts
cream cheese, mashed with
olives/chives/pimento

Pizza bits
Add <u>small</u> extras of your own choice
to <u>thin crust</u> ready/frozen pizza: bacon bits
                                                      olives, feta, etc.
Cook or heat pizza according to package directions.
Use kitchen shears or pizza wheel to cut into small pieces.

Party Cheese Ball
Mix or mash together until creamy: cream cheese
                                                    grated cheddar cheese
                                                    pickle bits or olive bits
                                                    a little Dijon or
                                                    dry mustard.
Form into a flattened ball and chill in plastic wrap.
Good with pita crisps, crackers, and veggies such as celery, cukes, pepper chunks.

Asian Avocado chunks:
Peel and cut into cubes   **firm** ripe avocado.
Immediately toss gently with   fresh lemon juice.
Then sprinkle with   extra-virgin olive oil
                                                  soy sauce
                                                   sesame seeds
                                                   S & P.
Serve with picks for easy spearing by guests.

Buttered Radishes:
Using   mild tasting radishes
cut each radish in half.
(If possible cut through the radishes vertically, leaving an inch or so of green top on each side.)
Paste halves back together with   sweet (not salted) butter.

Distinctive Dips

Thirty years ago dips were new and exciting. Here are some that you can easily make but not buy in every supermarket.

<u>Sweet and Sour Curry Dip</u>: Delicious with veggies, cold meats
<u>Gather together:</u>
1 T/**15ml** each Honey, Mustard, Curry Powder
1 C/**240ml** Mayo
1/8 t/**0.65ml** Cayenne Pepper
1 t/**5ml** fresh Lemon Juice

<u>Whisk and blend together</u>	honey, mustard curry powder.
Stir in and blend until smooth	mayo, cayenne, lemon juice.

Serve or cover and refrigerate.

<u>Chutney Cheddar Dip</u>: This is an unusual and substantial dip that looks fabulous. Serve it with crackers and veggies.
<u>Gather together:</u>
8 oz/**225g** Imperial Cheese (a small black tub with a red lid)
1/2 C/**120ml** Whipped Cream Cheese
2 T/**30ml** minced Green Onions
1/3 C/**80ml** chopped Chutney (such as mango)
1 small Pineapple, halved lengthwise and flesh cut out neatly
1/4 C/**60ml** coarsely chopped and toasted Almonds

<u>Beat together</u> until smooth and fluffy	imperial & cream cheeses.
Stir into the cheese	green onions chutney.
Spoon dip into	pineapple half.
Sprinkle overtop	almonds.
Surround pineapple and dip with	pineapple pieces.

Garlic Bread with Herbs

This savoury bread is wonderful with salads and soups for a company lunch and with stews or grilled fish and meats for dinner. You save money and add flavour by making this yourself instead of buying a frozen loaf.

Gather together:
1/2 C/**120ml** Soft Butter
2 Garlic cloves, chopped and minced
4 Basil leaves, sliced and chopped
2 stems Parsley, Leaves chopped fine
1 French Bread loaf, **unsliced**

Make the garlic butter:
Mix together with a fork   soft butter
                                 garlic
                                 basil
                                 parsley.

If possible, let the flavours
meld together for an hour.

Prepare the bread, butter it and bake at 350F/180C:
Cut off each end and then slice   bread loaf
in half horizontally.
Spread each half with   butter.
Place the halves on a baking
pan, butter sides up.
Bake, uncovered, for 10 - 20
minutes, until nicely browned.
Slice the toast thickly and serve
in a basket covered with a napkin.

Jazzed Up Pizzas

Here are a number of additional toppings that will jazz up a store-bought pizza or create a special one using any kind of bread base.

Your own toppings will create a delicious pizza from the bottom up when you begin with any of these as a base:
English muffins, split
Flatbreads, small or large
Pitas, split or left whole
Frozen bread dough
Frozen pizza shells
Frozen pizza dough, defrosted, spread thin and pre-baked for 5 mins for added crispness.

Note:
DRIZZLE EACH BASE WITH OLIVE OIL!

TIP! If you use unrefrigerated pizza shells, you will likely have a dry base.

Topping suggestions:
Onions, chopped – white/yellow/green
Garlic cloves, minced or sliced
Green/red/yellow Peppers and Jalapeño/Chilis, chopped
Olives, halved
Pesto
Tomatoes, sliced or chopped
Cheese, shredded, sliced, grated – Feta, Italian, Cheddar, etc.
Tomato-based sauces/salsas/chili
Broccoli and Cauliflower bits
Mushroom slices
Cooked Chicken/Ham/Sausage/Salami/Pepperoni
Uncooked Shrimp
Anchovies, chopped or not

Herbs – practically any variety or combinations you like: fresh chives, rosemary, parsley and sage chopped together
OR dried oregano, crushed fennel seeds, mixed 'Italian' herbs
Pineapple slices or bits
Mango slices
Seedless Grapes, halved
Cherries, pitted and halved
Apricot and Peach slices
Figs, quartered
Coconut chips
Chocolate or butterscotch bits

Note: THE LAST TOPPING MIGHT BE LIQUID HONEY!

Bake your pizza at 425-450F/220-230C:
In a hot toaster oven or regular oven
10 to 15 mins, directly on the rack.

TIP! Baking the pizza in the oven without a pan makes crisp crusts, but also messy ovens. If you use a pan, try heating it in the hot oven first, then sliding the pizza onto the pan. An oven safe skillet, upside down, makes a great pizza pan.

Or

Special Equipment: A pizza stone helps to cook the bottom of the pizza's base. The stone is pre-heated in the hot oven.

TIP! If you are puzzled about how to cut the pizza and you don't have a cutting wheel, use large scissors. They work quickly and cleanly.

Grilled Sandwiches   SKILLET/ EL.WOK/FRYPAN

Panini presses are the popular machines for grilled sandwiches today. Fifty years ago every new household had a convertible flat or ridged grilling machine to do the same thing… plus ca change! For this recipe all you really need is a basic skillet.

Gather together:
Hearty Bread sliced at least 1/4"/**.07cm thick** or Rolls such as Italian or Ciabatta, **cut in half lengthwise**
Mayonnaise
Mustard and/or Chutney
Cheese, **your choice** including cheddar, brie, havarti, blue
and/or Meat, **your choice** including cooked chicken, beef, ham, salami, tuna, shrimp
thin slices of Veg or Fruit such as tomato, sweet onion, sprouts, apple, mango, pineapple
Soft Butter
Garnish: Pickles or Olives

Build and prepare to Grill:

On each plain slice spread	mayo and/or mustard/chutney.
On one slice of each sandwich place and/or	thin layer of cheese meat
and apply another thin layer of	mayo/ mustard/chutney.
Add	veg and/or fruit.

Put the two roll/bread pieces together.
Butter the outside of the top slice.

Easy grilling:
Holding it together with
both hands, place in a med-hot pan/
el.wok/frypan, buttered side down the sandwich;
then lightly butter the outside of the
unbuttered roll/bread slice.
Place a pan/can on top of the
sandwich to act as a press and cover.
Turn heat to med-low
and fry for 4-5 mins (2-3 in el.wok/frypan),
checking for browning.
When the bottom is a lovely golden,
use a wide spatula to flip the sandwich.
Do not replace the 'cover'.
Let the bottom brown, 1-3 mins.
Remove each sandwich to a warm plate.
Presentation:
Using a sharp straight knife, cut the
sandwich into triangular halves/thirds.
Garnish: A snazzy garnish is a
coloured pick or toothpick spearing a pickle or olive
to each sandwich section.

Make-a meal: Restaurants usually offer 'salad or fries' with grilled sandwiches. At home you can make sure your sandwich includes veggies. If you feel you want more carbs, sweet potato 'fries' would be a good choice. The frozen variety is tasty these days. Of course, for ease and crunch, about 10 potato chips do the job nicely.

Your Own Hamburger SKILLET/ EL.WOK/FRYPAN

Most of us like burgers, especially those made with beef. There are so many hamburger variations; you'll want to determine which one(s) you like best. Here are some suggestions. Amounts below make 2 burgers.

Gather together:
1/2-2/3 lb/**225-330g** Ground Beef, preferably lean
2 T/**30ml** minced Onion
1 T/**15ml** Worcestershire Sauce
1 T/**15ml** dry Bread crumbs
S & P
2 dashes Olive Oil
Optional: 2 1"/**2.25cm** chunks Blue Cheese
              1 slice Bacon, cooked to crisp, crumbled
              2 slices Cheddar Cheese
2 Hamburg Buns, preferably soft, and whole wheat for nutrients

Mix burger ingredients together:
In a bowl **gently** mix together   beef, onion
                                          Worcestershire,
                                          crumbs, S & P

and gently form mixture into 2 equal
patties, about 3/4"/**1.9cm** thick.
If using optional ingredients:
Make an indentation in each patty
and press in to cover either/or   blue cheese/bacon.
Spread over each patty on both sides   olive oil.
Grill the patties:
On a med-hot skillet/el.wok/frypan, grill   patties
4 mins (3 for el.wok/frypan) on first side.
Turn patties over and grill another
3 mins to cook through.

If using, place on cooked patty   cheese slice
just before removing patties from grill.
Warm the buns:
Meanwhile, toast   split buns
OR
warm them in a micro, 30 secs
OR toast them in a toaster oven/el. wok.
Build your burger:
The variety of condiments is endless.
Below are some suggestions:

sliced tomatoes	sliced red onions	sliced pickles
shredded lettuce	any mustard	any relish
avocado slices	pickled beets	pickled peppers
pepper slices	shredded carrots	fresh herbs
ketchup/chow-chow/chili sauce		mayonnaise

TIP! A patty made with 4 oz/115g meat is big enough for most people. The super-sized burgers sold by some chains ought to be renamed fat burgers. We are better off eating 2 normal sized burgers with their whole wheat buns and veggie condiments than scarfing down one bun crammed with too much meat.

TIP! The commercial burger world generally creates thin patties, about 1/4"/.65cm so the meat cooks quickly and thoroughly. At home, the patties can be thicker provided they are cooked sufficiently.

TIP! You will note the word "gentle" in this recipe. Too much pressure on the ground meat ruins the patty's tenderness and flavour. The inherent fat cannot run around inside a patty that has been pounded into a puck.

Hammy Cheese Croissant MICRO

Here is a guide to a fun and tasty hot sandwich for 1. It's quick too because it's zapped in the microwave. Remember to micro one sandwich at a time.

Gather together:
1 Croissant, slit lengthwise
1/4 C/**60ml** shredded Cheese
1/8 C/**30ml** diced Ham
1 T/**15ml** Sour Cream
1 t/**5ml** Mayonnaise
1/2 t/ **2.5ml** Prepared Mustard
2 slices Tomato, diced

Mix and stuff :
In a bowl combine all ingredients except croissant.

Stuff the filling into the croissant.

Micro:
Place the sandwich on a flat dish and cover it with a paper towel. Micro on HIGH for 1 min, then test the filling for heat. Maybe micro for another 30 secs.

TIP! This recipe works well without the ham but with crabmeat, chicken shreds or cooked bacon bits.

TIP! Croissants heated in a micro oven will not retain their crisp crust. So use the supermarket soft crust variety for this sandwich. (Save real bakery croissants for a swell brunch with friends. Those should be heated gently in a 250-300F/120-150C oven.)

Your Own Hot Dog SKILLET/MICRO/TOASTER OVEN/ EL.WOK/FRYPAN

Choosing the best dog is a problem these days. The quantities of fillers and sodium in some are truly scary. Kosher franks seem to be the tastiest for adults but perhaps a little too flavourful for children. There are many ways to cook the dogs... use whatever equipment you have.

Gather together:
1 Weiner/Frankfurter
1 Bun, preferably soft whole wheat, buttered or not
Paper Towels for microwaving
OR
Skillet/micro/el.wok-frypan/toaster oven+ **splash of liquid**
(liquid could be water, beer, even wine)
Optional condiments:

chopped onion	chopped tomato	mustard
shredded lettuce	shredded cheese	any relish
ketchup	chow-chow	chili sauce
warmed chili con carne		warmed sauerkraut

Prepare the condiments:
Chop up and/or heat your choice of   condiments.
Heat up weiner/frank and bun:
Heat in skillet/micro/toaster oven/el.wok   frank
3mins/1 min/5 mins/2-3 mins respectively.
Heat in micro/toaster-oven/el. wok   bun
30 sec/3 mins/2 mins respectively or
in a <u>dry</u> skillet, toast bun about 1 min.
Put it all together and enjoy!

TIP! When you're making hot dogs for the gang, use a combination of water and beer for the heating liquid. You'll be amazed at the extra burst of flavour!

Triscuit Toppers

The makers of Triscuits are marketing them as a healthy snack food. They are full of fiber, low in saturated fat and fairly low in sodium, especially the newer varieties. A great vehicle for canapé toppings!

<u>Gather together:</u>
4-6 Triscuits **per serving**
Mayo mixed with Mustard – grainy, Dijon or other type
<u>Selection of toppers, **baked**</u>:

* Salami slices, garnished with Cheese
* Cheddar Cheese squares with Strawberry slices & ground Pepper
* broiled Red Pepper slices with Black Olive bits
* Goat Cheese with Pineapple bits
* Sun dried Tomatoes sprinkled with Parmesan and/or cooked Bacon bits
* Cheddar or Mozzarella Cheese & cooked Bacon bits

<u>Bake on a tray</u> in a 350F/180C oven 10 mins.
Serve on a platter garnished with Parsley and Pickles.

Selection of **uncooked** toppers:

* Blue Cheese with thin Celery slices
* Slice of cooked Egg with a dab of Mayo and Green Onion bits
* an Apple slice with a dab of Boursin cheese
* Sliced Cherry Tomatoes with Mozzarella bits
* Cream Cheese with Chutney
* Cream Cheese with Pineapple bits
* Cream Cheese with a Pickle slice
* Smoked salmon with Red Onion bits & chopped Capers

Serve on a tray garnished with Celery and Carrot sticks, Pickles and Olives.

TIP! Do not prepare the uncooked toppers more than 30 mins or so before serving time so the triscuit retains its crispness instead of becoming soggy. (Baked triscuits with toppers do not have this problem.)

TIP! Grocery stores now feature olives at a decent price. Try a variety, especially the mixed small size and the large green and black olives with peppers.

Zippy Tortilla Nachos

OVEN/TOASTER OVEN EL.WOK/FRYPAN

Simple and simply great for the gang, especially with beer!

Gather together:
Veg oil for the oven tray or wok's/frypan's surface
bag of Nacho Chips
Refried Beans from a **can**
jar of Salsa, mild or medium hot
bag of Shredded Mozzarella, Monterey Jack or Cheddar

Pile, Dab, Sprinkle:
Turn on your broiler/oven/el.wok/frypan.
On a greased tray (wok surface) spread   nacho chips.
Dab each chip with   beans, salsa.
Sprinkle over all   the cheese.

Make the nachos hot:
To melt cheese, place under the
broiler for 2-3 mins. Watch!
OR
Bake in a hot oven, 450-475F/230-240C
For about 5 mins... watching!
OR
Bake directly on the wok's surface,
lid on, low to med heat, 5-6 mins.

TIP! To make a meal out of your nachos, you could spread on a bit of cooked hamburger or sausage meat before the cheese.

Sweet Things

Baked Apples for 2	122
Light & Tasty Cheesecakes	123
Dream Cake	124
Amazing Alaska Party Cake	126
Quick Cake Desserts	128
Charlotte's Spice Cake	129
Ice Cream Toppers	130
Bread and Fruit Pudding	131
Lemon Snow Pudding	132
Drunken Grapes – a Company Dessert	133
Quick Pastry and Tender Crusts	134
Fruit Pie with Crumble Topping	136
Lemon Curd Tarts	137

Baked Apples for 2

This is an easy and lovely dessert at any time of year, especially when the baked apples are topped with vanilla ice cream.

Gather together:
2 large Apples, Empire or Granny Smith that hold together when cooked
handful of Raisins
Brown Sugar, 1 T/**15ml for each** apple
Cinnamon, a **dash for each** apple
Butter, 2 t/**10ml** for each apple
1 Lemon
Optional: Ice Cream

Prepare the apples for baking:
Core the apples from the flower end but do not peel. If you have a melon baller, use it to finish the job of coring.

Into a buttered oven pan place	cored apples.
Almost fill the apple centres with	raisins
and top the raisins with	brown sugar.
Sprinkle with a	dash of cinnamon.
Top with	butter.
Squeeze over each apple	fresh lemon juice.

Bake the apples at 350F/180C:
for 45 mins to 1 hour.

Spoon over the apples	the gooey juices.
Serve the apples warm with	ice cream

TIP! Why not bake apples when you have the oven on for another use? Then refrigerate and reheat later.

Light & Tasty Cheesecakes
Perfect for a party! Makes 10-12 servings.

Gather together:
2 ready-made Crumb Crusts
2 C/480ml low fat Cottage Cheese, fine curd
8 oz/225g plain Cream Cheese, room temp
1/4 C/60ml Sugar
1 Lemon, zest & juice
pinch Salt
2 t/10ml Vanilla
Optional: Topping of **1 C**/240ml Sour Cream mixed with
1/4 C/60ml Sugar

Break up to loosen crumbs and repress into crusts:
Prepare **2** pie plates by greasing lightly.
Break up the ready-made crusts and divide
crumbs into two pie plates – no kidding!
Press onto bottoms of pie plates   crumbs.

Prepare filling:
Whiz in Blender or Processor   all ingredients
except sour cream/sugar mixture.
Pour filling into   each crust.
Bake about 35 mins at 350F/180C:
until centre is <u>almost</u> set. (For a cake
that does not crack, place pie plates
in a bain marie (a larger pan containing
hot water half-way up pie plate sides.)
Chill baked cakes.
<u>OR</u>
If desired, top with   sour cream & sugar
and bake another 10 mins.

Dream Cake

If you like coconut desserts, this moist cake is for you. It's that simple even for non-bakers.

Gather together:
1/2 C/120ml soft Butter
1/4 C/60ml Brown Sugar **plus another 1 1/2 C**/360ml Brown Sugar
1 C/240ml Flour **plus another 2 rounded T**/30+ml Flour
2 Eggs
1/2 t/2.5ml BP
1 C/240ml Nuts, chopped and toasted
1 C/240ml shredded or desiccated Coconut, unsweetened
8x8"/20x20cm pan lined with wax paper or foil and buttered. Make sure the lining overhangs the pan on all 4 sides for easy unmoulding of the cake.

Make Layer 1:
Cream together with an electric beater	butter **1/4 C**/60ml brown sugar.
Beat in on low speed speed	**1 C**/240ml flour.
Pat the mixture into	prepared pan.

Make Layer 2:
Beat lightly in a clean bowl	eggs.
Beat in on medium	**1 1/2 C**/360mL brown sugar.
In a separate bowl, whisk together	**2 round T**/30ml flour BP.
Stir the flour mixture into the egg mixture or beat in at low speed.	
Stir in	nuts, coconut.

Pour the dough on top of the first
layer and smooth it lightly.
<u>Bake at 300F/150C:</u>
20-30 mins until a toothpick
comes out almost clean.
Let the cake rest on a rack until cool.
Unmould the cake using the
overhanging wax paper or tin foil.

TIP! For baking, make sure your eggs are at room temp. That takes about an hour out of the fridge.

TIP! Sometimes brown sugar is kept in the pantry for quite a while. If so, it can become rock hard. What to do? For immediate softening, put the hard sugar and a dampened paper towel in a micro safe plastic bag and micro for 20 secs or so. The best way to avoid the problem is to keep a dampened clay disc in a sealed container with the sugar. The discs are cheap and can be found in grocery and food equipment stores.

Amazing Alaska Party Cake

This cake serves 12. It is easy to make since little cooking is involved. It's fun to serve and eat too. The recipe seems long but it's a cinch to create...just have plenty of counter space.

Gather together:
1 frozen Chocolate loaf Cake
1 frozen contrasting flavour/colour loaf/brick Cake
1 Brick* of contrasting Ice Cream (ice cream IS sold in bricks!)
10 Eggs at room temperature
1 1/2 C/360ml White Sugar
Wax Paper, Electric Mixer, Baking Sheet

Cut!
Working quickly to keep the cakes
and ice cream hard,
on wax paper, cut in half horizontally   each cake
and
on wax paper, cut in thirds horizontally   ice cream brick.

Assemble the party cake:
On the baking sheet assemble the Alaska in this order (making sure that any cake layer with icing on it does not have its icing on the very bottom or very top of the layered Alaska):
1. layer of chocolate cake
2. layer of ice cream
3. layer of contrasting cake
4. layer of ice cream
5. layer of contrasting cake
6. layer of ice cream
7. layer of chocolate cake

Return the party cake to the freezer.

Make the Meringue:
Separate, one at a time** from yolks,   the egg whites
by breaking each egg into a dish, then
pouring each egg through your
outstretched fingers into a   large mixing bowl
enabling the whites to flow down into bowl.
(Store yolks, with a layer of water on top,
in an open jar in the fridge up to 3 days)
Beat on high until foamy   egg whites
and gradually beat in   the sugar.
Continue beating until the whites
form stiff peaks when the beaters
are lifted. This is meringue!

Complete the party cake:
Spread over the frozen cake   meringue
making sure that the meringue
encases the cake completely,
right down to the baking sheet.

Bake at 475F/250C:
about 3 mins until the meringue
just turns golden.
Serve immediately.

TIP! Decorate with Sparklers for more fun.

*TIP! If you cannot find ice cream in brick form, just make your own brick. Soften a container of ice cream, then repack the ice cream into a loaf pan that has been lined with wax paper, edges overhanging. Refreeze. Lift the brick out of the pan using the overhanging paper and peel off the paper.

**TIP! By first breaking each egg into a dish you avoid contaminating all the eggs should one smell less than fresh.

Quick Cake Desserts

These toppers turn store-bought cakes into special desserts. Use pound, sponge cake or angel food cake. Keep unused cake in the freezer, well wrapped, for 3 months.

Creamy Fruit Sauce for Cake
Mix together in a small bowl

1 C/240ml Sour Cream
1/3 C/80ml Brown Sugar
1 C/240ml Berries/small Ripe Fruit, sliced Grapes.

Spoon sauce over slices of pound, sponge or angel cake.

Sweet & Sour Sauce for Cake
Mix together in a small bowl

3 T/45ml Jam
2 T/30ml Heavy Cream, whipped
1/2 t Vanilla
Juice of **1/2** Lemon or Lime.

Spoon over cake or spread between slices of cake.

Yogurt Fruit Sauce for Cake
Mix together in a small bowl

1 C/240ml Plain or Vanilla Yogurt
1 T/15ml Brown Sugar
Juice of **1** Orange
1 T Orange Zest

Spoon over cake slices.

Charlotte's Spice Cake

Years ago every cook had a recipe that depended on a can of condensed tomato soup. This one is Charlotte's.

Gather together:
1/2 C/120ml soft Butter
1 C/240ml Sugar
2 Eggs, yolks separated from whites
1 1/2C/360ml Flour
3/4 t/3.75ml S
2 t/10ml BS
1/2 t/2.5ml **each** ground Cinnamon, ground Cloves, ground Allspice, ground Nutmeg
10 oz can Condensed Tomato Soup
1/2 C/120ml chopped Nuts – walnuts, pecans or almonds
1 C/240ml Raisins

Use your electric mixer, then your wooden spoon:
Beat together with mixer adding sugar gradually.	butter & sugar,
Add and beat until mixed in	egg yolks.
Whisk together	flour, S, BS, spices.
With the spoon beat the flour mixture into <u>alternately</u> with thirds of the can of finishing with	butter mixture tomato soup, the flour.
Beat with mixer until soft peaks form	egg whites.
Fold beaten whites into	batter.
Stir in	nuts, raisins.

Spoon the batter into an 8"/20cm pan lined with <u>greased</u> wax paper.
Bake at 350F/180C:
45 mins, when a toothpick comes out clean. Let rest 10 mins on a rack.

Ice Cream toppers

Toffee Apples or Bananas

Gather together:
2-3 T/30-45ml Butter
2-3 T/30-45ml Sugar
11-2 Granny apples, cored, or firm Bananas, sliced across

Turning the ingredients into toffee:
Gently melt in med saucepan   butter.
Add and cook on med until dissolved   sugar.
Stir in   fruit
cooking on med-low until fruit pieces
are 'toffeed' on all sides.

Maple Nut Syrup

Gather together:
1/2 C/**120ml** Maple Syrup
1/4 C/**60ml** Pecans, Walnuts or Almonds toasted, using med heat, shaking pan to prevent burning, about 5 mins

Heat and Stir:
In the micro, on HIGH, 30 secs, heat   syrup.
Stir in   toasted nuts.
Reheat in the micro on HIGH 30 secs.
Enjoy over your favourite ice cream

Bread and Fruit Pudding – a method recipe

This method recipe gives you the idea for a sweet, not savoury, bread pudding. It's really good and it's easy to prepare!

Gather together:
a small to medium Baking Dish, buttered
2 Slices of Bread such as raisin, egg or firm white, torn into 1/2"/**1.25cm** pieces
2 small Fruits, sliced or diced, such as apple, pear, peach, plum, banana, etc.
1-2 T/**15-30ml** Butter, cut into bits
Custard ingredients, below

In a mixing bowl whisk together:

1 Egg
2/3 C/**160ml** Milk
1/8 C/**30ml** Sugar
1/4 t/**1.25ml** Cinnamon
1/8 t/**0.65ml** each ground Ginger and ground Nutmeg
pinch S

Put the pudding together:
Cover bottom of the baking dish with one-half of the bread pieces.

Cover the bread with fruit.
Pour over one-half of the custard.
Cover that with remaining bread.
Pour over the remaining custard.
Dot all over with the butter bits.
Bake at 375F/190C:
30-40 mins, until top puffs and fruit is soft.
Let pudding sit 5-10 mins before serving.

Lemon Snow Pudding

This is an old comfort food dessert. It is simple to prepare, light, and so lovely to eat.

Gather together:
3 T/45ml Cornstarch mixed with **2/3 C**/160ml white Sugar
1/2 t/2.5ml S
1 1/2 C/360ml Boiling Water
2 Lemons, juice and grated zest
2 Egg Whites

Cook, stirring:
In a heavy saucepan on med, cook	cornstarch, sugar, salt, water
stirring until mixture thickens. Remove from heat and let cool.	

Add the lemon and the snow:
Stir in	lemon juice grated zest.
Beat together until stiff	egg whites.
Using a rubber spatula, fold whites into	lemon cornstarch mixture.

Pour the pudding into a serving dish, preferably glass to show the colours.

TIP! To separate egg yolks from whites, crack an egg into your hand and allow whites to drip through your fingers. It works!

TIP! To 'fold', run the rubber spatula down one side, across the bottom and up the other side, thus bringing the ingredients together without stirring.

Drunken Grapes – a Company Dessert

This recipe may sound weird but the result is a tasty and colourful dessert. Be sure to serve it in glass goblets.

Gather together:
4 handfuls Seedless Grapes, halved if large
3 T/45ml Brown Sugar
1/4 C/60ml Vodka
4 T/60ml Crème Fraiche (supermarket) or Sour Cream
1/2 C/120ml slivered Almonds, toasted

Make the grapes drunk:
Toss together, then refrigerate 6 hrs   grapes
                                             sugar
                                             vodka.

When ready to serve:
Stir in   crème fraiche/
                                             sour cream.

Spoon grapes **loosely** into glasses.
Top each glass with   almonds.

Serve with thin wafer cookies – almond, vanilla, chocolate – your choice.

Food Processor Quick Pastry & Tender Crusts

The Quick Pastry recipe below, using oil, is suitable for a one-crust pie or as a base for bar or squares recipes. The following note entitled "Tender Pastry Crusts" refers to recipes using shortening, butter or lard, not oil, as the fat.

Gather together:
1/2 C/120ml Whole Wheat all-purpose Flour
1 C/240ml Cake & Pastry Flour
1/4 t/1.25ml S
2 t/10ml Sugar
3/8 C/90ml cubed hard Butter
1/4 C/60ml Vegetable Oil such as Canola
1 T/15ml Vodka if you have it
(Note that the vodka moistens the dough but does not combine with its protein, thus creating a tender pastry.)
2-3 T/30-45ml Ice Water

Pulse together in a processor: all dry ingredients.
Add: cubed hard butter, vegetable oil

and pulse to consistency of large crumbs.
Sprinkle over top   vodka,
   2 T ice water.

Pulse to combine, adding additional   1 T ice water
if necessary, until mixture forms a
ragged dough that holds together
when squeezed by your fingertips.

No need to refrigerate this dough – just carry on with your pie or bars, according to the following steps:

For a pie dough follow these steps:
1. The dough is crumbly but, between sheets of plastic wrap or wax paper, it can be rolled and patted to form about a 10"/25cm circle. Then remove the top paper.
2. Transfer the dough to a pie tin by dumping it upside down into the tin. Then remove the other paper.
3. Using palms and fingers press the dough up the sides and over the base to create an even crust. Pinch around the edge between two fingers to make an attractive flute.
4. Cover the pie crust with plastic wrap while making the filling.

Tender Pastry Crusts
There are many ways to make pastry – depending on the fat(s) and many more ways to create a never-fail tender dough. One tenderizing method is to use one beaten egg plus one teaspoon of lemon juice as part of the liquid. The total liquid, with added ice water, should then be **1/4 C**/60ml. Methods of mixing and handling the dough also matter. The cooks of *Canadian Living* magazine recommend mixing/processing just to the 'ragged' stage. That means the dough does not yet form a ball but it will stick together when pressed between floured hands.

Golden Pastry Crusts: Even though most recipes and oven instructions advise you to bake pastries in the centre of the oven, fully browning/cooking the bottom of a pie can be a problem. If you use a glass pie plate you can inspect the bottom crust. If the bottom is pale/undercooked at the 3/4 stage of baking time, move the pastry to the bottom rack. If so, you may need to lightly cover the pie's top crust edge to keep it from over-browning. Use metal pie rings that fit around the pastry edge to prevent burning or simply put strips of foil around the edge of the top crust to protect it.

Fruit Pie with Crumble Topping
For pies, the main concerns are sweetness/tartness and thickening of the filling. Success depends on the fruit's quality. See the bottom of the page for baking temps and times.

Apple Filling
<u>Mix together all ingredients except Butter:</u>
5-6 C/1.2-1.45L pared, cored, sliced Apple
1/3-1/2 C/80-120ml Sugar
1 1/2-2 T/23-30ml Flour
1/2 t/2.5ml Cinnamon
pinch Nutmeg
Dump into shell the filling.
Top filling with **2 T**/30ml Butter, cut into small pieces.

Berry Filling
<u>Follow instructions for Apple, above, using these ingredients:</u>
4 C/1L Berries (drained well and <u>1 C/**240ml** more if frozen</u>)
1/2-1 C/120-240ml Sugar: stir into fruit and taste while adding
2 T/30ml Flour + **1 T**/15ml Cornstarch + **1/2 t**/2.5ml Cinnamon, all mixed together then stirred into the fruit

Crumble Topping for Crisps, Pies, Desserts
<u>Gather together:</u>
3/4 C/180ml rolled Oats & **3/4 C**/180ml Sugar
1/2 C/120ml Flour
1 t/5ml Cinnamon
1/4 t/1.25ml Nutmeg & **1/4 t**/1.25ml S
3/8 C/**3 oz**/90g Cold Butter, cut into 9 bits
Pulse together to an even size all ingredients.
Spread topping over filling.
<u>Bake 45-60 mins at 375/190C:</u>
until filling is tender and top is golden.

Lemon Curd Tarts

Especially in the spring, nothing beats the fresh taste of lemon curd! It's a thick creamy filling and there is a grocery store variety. But it does not compare with the home-made version.

Gather together:
3 Egg Yolks (save whites in the fridge a couple of days)
3/4 C/180ml Sugar
1 1/2 t/7.5ml Lemon zest
1/2 C/120ml Lemon Juice
1/4 C/60ml Butter, cut into bits
about 12 tart shells (home made or frozen pastry)
Fresh Berries and/or Whipped Cream as garnish

A simple cooking process:
In a medium saucepan, combine	egg yolks, sugar.
Add	lemon zest, juice.
Cook on medium-low, stirring, 8 minutes or until mixture coats the back of a metal spoon. Remove from heat.	
Add and stir in to melt	butter bits.
Cover curd with a piece of waxed paper to prevent crusting. Refrigerate until just set.	

Fill and Garnish tarts:
Fill baked tart shells with and just before serving	curd
garnish with	berries and whipped cream.

INDEX

Amazing Alaska Party Cake		126
Anne's Waldorf Salad for 2		52
Apples, Baked, for 2		122
Apple and Sweet Potato Bake		25
'Asian' Chili Chicken		67
Asparagus Spears for 1		26
Bacon & Bean Quesadillas		94
Baked Apples for 2		122
Baked Egg Plus on Toast		3
Bare Bones Kitchen Equipment		viii
Basic Supplies		xv
BBQ Chicken, Creative Uses for		70
Beans	Better Baked Beans	64
	Mixed Bean Soup	24
Beef	Beefsteak Casserole, Beginners	65
	Beef Stroganoff, Instant	66
	Beef Chili Quesadillas	95
	Meatballs, Saucy	90
	Your Own Hamburger	114
Beets, Glazed		27
Beth's Best Salmon Fillet		97
BLT, Breakfast		2
Blue Cheese Iceberg Wedges		46
Bread and Fruit Pudding		131
Bread, Garlic with Herbs		109
BREAKFAST		1-16
Broccoli, Chinese Orange for 4		28
Buttery Garlic Chicken Breasts for 2		68
Cake	Amazing Alaska Party Cake	126
	Cheesecakes, Light & Tasty	123
	Cake Desserts, Quick	128
	Dream Cake	124
	Ice Cream Toppers	130
	Spice Cake, Charlotte's	129
Cake Sauce	Creamy Fruit	128
	Sweet & Sour	128
	Yogurt Fruit	128

Canapés/hors d'oeuvres, Easy		106
Carrot Salad or Slaw		48
Carrots, Candied		29
Charlotte's Spice Cake		129
Cheesecakes, Light & Tasty		123
Cheese Sauce		54
Chicken	BBQ Chicken, Creative Uses for	70
	Caesar Salad for 1+	49
	Chicken Breasts, Buttery Garlic, for 2	68
	Chicken Breasts, 'Italian', for 2	72
	Chicken Stew, 'French' for 2	78
	Chili Chicken,' Asian', for 2	67
	Curried Chicken, Noodley, for 1	69
	Parmesan Chicken, Murielle's, for 4	74
	Roasted Chicken for 1	75
	Roast Chicken, Chinese-style for 4	76
	Southern Fried Chicken for 4	77
Chili Beef Quesadillas		95
Chinese-style Roast Chicken for 4		76
Cioppino, Fish & Seafood for 2		83
Corn-on-the-Cob, Micro'd, Mary's		30
Condiment Fixer-Uppers		45
Croissant, Hammy Cheese		116
Cukes and Peppers, Micro'd		31
Dips, Distinctive		108
Dream Cake		124
Dressing, Blue Cheese on Iceberg Wedges		46
Drunken Grapes – a Company Dessert		133
Dumplings, Soups & Stews		62
Easy Canapés/hors d'oeuvres		106
Eggs	Baked on Toast	3
	Frittata with Toast	86
	Hard Boiled, Perfect	4
	Poached, Perfect	5
	Omelet, Easy	10
	Scrambled, Perfect	6
	Soft Boiled, Perfect	7
	with Hash	8
Electric Woks/Frypans		xii

ENTRÉES			63-104
Kitchen Equipment		vi - viii	
Fish	Foiled Fish		82
	Pan Fried Fillets		80
	Fish Pot Pie		84
	Fish & Seafood Cioppino for 2		83
Flavour Enhancers and Aromatics, TIPS			21-24
Foiled Fish			82
'French' Chicken Stew for 2			78
French Toast			9
Frittata with Toast			86
Fruit Pie with Crumble Topping			136
Garlic Bread with Herbs			109
Good Things Salad			50
Grapes, Drunken – a Company Dessert			133
Gravy, Your Own			55
Grilled Sandwiches			112
Hamburger, Your Own			114
Hammy Cheese Croissant			116
Hearty Pea and Sausage Soup			60
Ice Cream Toppers			130
Imperial to Metric Equivalents		xviii	
INDEX			138-142
Inspiration		iv	
Instant Garlic Shrimp			100
'Italian' Chicken Breasts for 2			72
Jazzed Up Pizzas			110
John's Fried Scallops with Dill Sauce			98
Kitchen Tips for the Beginner, TIPS		ix -- x	
Hot Dog, Your own			117
Lemon Snow Pudding			132
Lemon Curd Tarts			137
Light & Tasty Cheesecakes			123
List of Terms/Abbreviations		xv - xvi	
Liver 'n Onions for 2			88
Lobster and Avocado Cocktail			44
Mashed Potatoes, Garlic with Milk			32
Meatballs, Saucy, for Company			90
Metric/Imperial Conversions		xviii	

Mixed Bean Soup		58
Nachos, Zippy Tortilla		120
Noodley Curried Chicken for 1		69
Old Fashioned Tuna Casserole		104
Omelet, Easy		10
Onion Soup, Old-style, for 2		59
Oven Temperatures		xi - xii
Pancakes, Anne's Blueberry for 4		12
Pan Fried Fish Fillets		80
Parmesan Chicken, Murielle's for 4		74
Party Cake, Amazing Alaska		126
Pastry	Quick (Food Processor)	134
	Tender Crusts	135
Perfect Blue Cheese Dressing		46
Perfect Poached Egg		4
Perfect Hard Boiled Egg		5
Perfect Scrambled Egg		6
Perfect Soft Boiled Egg		7
Pie, Fruit with Crumble Topping		136
Pizzas, Jazzed Up		110
Pork	Chops, Spicy Glazed for 2	91
	Roasted	92
	Roasted Garlic	93
	Sausage Supper for 1	102
	Spareribs, Simple Saucy	103
Potatoes	Garlic Mashed, with Milk	32
	Mediterranean Roasted	33
	Scalloped, Real, for 1-2	34
	Sweet Potato Hash Browns for 2	35
Porridge, Your Own Oatmeal		13
Pudding	Bread and Fruit	131
	Lemon Snow	132
Quesadillas	Bacon & Bean	94
	Chili Beef	95
Quick Cake Desserts		128
Quick Tomato Sauce, Anne's		56
Rice	Rice, with Peas and Herbs	37
	Rice, Orange	36
	Rice, Sweet and Savoury	38

Roasted Chicken for 1		75
Roasted Garlic Pork		93
Roasted Pork		92
Salad	Blue Cheese Iceberg Wedges	46
	Carrot Salad or Slaw	48
	Chicken Caesar Salad for 1+	49
	Crunchy Salad, Whole Meal for 1	53
	Good Things Salad	50
	Lobster and Avocado Cocktail	44
	Tomato Salad for 2	51
	Waldorf Salad, Anne's for 2	52
Salmon	Fillet, Beth's Best	97
	Salmon in the Micro	96
Salty and Sweet Shrimp for 2		101
Sandwiches	BLT, Breakfast	2
	Croissant, Hammy Cheese	116
	Eggy, 2	16
	Grilled	112
	Hamburger, Your Own	114
	Hot Dog, Your Own	117
SANDWICHES AND SNACKS		105-120
Sauces	Cheese Sauce	54
	Condiments, Speedy Fixer-Uppers	45
	Tomato Sauce, Quick, Anne's	56
	Your Own Sauce/Gravy	55
SALADS, SAUCES AND SOUPS		43-62
Saucy Meatballs for Company		90
Sausage Supper for 1		102
Scallops, John's Fried with Dill Sauce		98
Scalloped Potatoes, Real, for 1-2		34
Shrimp	Instant Garlic	100
	Salty and Sweet for 2	101
Southern Fried Chicken for 4		77
Soups	Mixed Bean	58
	Onion, Old-style, for 2	59
	Hearty Pea and Sausage	60
Spareribs, Simple Saucy		103
Spicy Glazed Pork Chops for 2		91
Steak (Beefsteak) Casserole, Beginners, for Company		65

Stroganoff, Beef, Instant for 1			66
Supplies, Basic		xv	
Sweet Potato Hash Browns for 2			35
SWEET THINGS			121-137
Tarts, Lemon Curd			137
Tender Pastry Crusts			135
Terms/Abbreviations		xvi – xvii	
TIPS	Basic Supplies	xv	
	Flavour Enhancers and Aromatics		21-24
	Kitchen Tips for the Beginner	ix – x	
	Oven Temperatures	xi – xii	
	Useful/and not Prepared Items	xiii – xiv	
	Veggies and Fruit		18-20
Tomato Salad for 2			51
Tomatoes, Baked			40
Tomato Sauce, Quick, Anne's			56
Triscuit Toppers			118
Tuna Casserole, Old Fashioned			104
Useful/and not Prepared Grocery Items		xiii – xiv	
Veggie and Fruit Tips			18-20
VEGETABLES & FRUIT			17-42
Veggies, Baked, for the Gang			41
Vinaigrette, Your Own			47
Waffles, Basil's Best Buttermilk			14
Waldorf Salad, Anne's for 2			52
Whole Meal Crunchy Salad for 1			53
Your Own Hamburger			114
Your Own Hotdog			117
Your Own Sauce/Gravy			55
Zippy Tortilla Nachos			120
Zucchini Boats, Baked for 2			42
2 Eggy Sandwiches			16

www.ingramcontent.com/pod-product-compliance
Lightning Source LLC
Chambersburg PA
CBHW070104080526
44586CB00013B/1180